WORD
GAME

Wilbert J. Levy

Dedicated to serving

AMSCO

our nation's youth

When ordering this book, please specify:
either N 452 W or WORD GAME.

AMSCO SCHOOL PUBLICATIONS, INC.
315 Hudson Street / New York, N.Y. 10013

Books by Wilbert J. Levy

More Powerful Reading
Poems: American Themes
Reading and Growing
Sentence Play
Wordplay
Paragraph Play
Word Game

Amsco Literature Program
    The Red Badge of Courage With Reader's Guide
    Treasure Island With Reader's Guide

Amsco Writing English Series
    Writing English: Foundations
    Paragraph Power
    Sense of Sentences
    Composition: Prewriting, Response, Revision

Pronunciations and Key to Pronunciation courtesy of
Scott, Foresman and Company. From SCOTT, FORESMAN
ADVANCED DICTIONARY by E. L. Thorndike and Clarence
L. Barnhart. Copyright © 1983 by Scott, Foresman
and Company. Reprinted by permission.

ISBN 0-87720-671-6

Printed in the United States of America

Contents

LESSON 1

LOOK AT THE PICTURE

What Did You See?

1. The man on the bicycle is angry. How can you tell? Give two ways.

   _____

   _____

2. What has probably made him angry?

   _____

3. How does the baby seem to feel?

   _____

4. The baby is holding what two things in his fists? What do these tell you?

_____

_____

5. Standing just behind the taxi is a woman with a bike. Give two or three reasons to believe that she is probably the wife of the man on the bike.

_____

_____

_____

6. Who do you think is right in this argument? Give your reasons.

_____

_____

_____

PRONUNCIATION

Here are ten lesson words suggested by the picture. With the help of your teacher, pronounce each word.

affection (ə fek′ shən)
dispute (dis pyüt′)
gesture (jes′ chər)
grasp (grasp)
peril (per′ əl)
proceed (prə sēd′)
protest (prə test′)
reckless (rek′ lis)
stationary (stā′ shə ner′ ē)
vehicle (vē′ə kəl)

SPELLING

Be sure you know how to spell each word. On the next page are the words given in sentences. Letters are missing from each word. First put the missing letters where they belong. Then write each complete word in the space.

1. Each one in the family had great AFFEC__ __ __N for everyone else in the family.

   1. _____

2. The D__ __PUTE between the batter and the umpire ended with the batter being thrown out of the game.

   2. _____

3. With a firm GE__ __ __RE, the police officer signaled the driver to stop.

   3. _____

4. The baby held the bottle in a tight GR__ __P until it was empty, then calmly dropped it on the floor.

   4. _____

5. Drivers were warned about the P__R__L of the icy roads.

   5. _____

6. The game was so boring that the fans left their seats and began to PRO__ __ __D to the exits long before it was over.

   6. _____

7. Although people P__ __TEST against the high cost of food, the costs keep going up.

   7. _____

8. The R__ __ __LESS person dashed across the street against a red light.

   8. _____

9. Amidst all the movement of tugboats and ships in the harbor, the Statue of Liberty stood, STA__ __ON__RY and majestic.

   9. _____

10. The covered wagon was the VEH__C__ __ used by the pioneer families in their westward journey.

    10. _____

How Do These Words Go With the Picture?

How well can you see the connection between each word and the picture? For as many words as you can, explain briefly how the word goes with the picture. To help you, three of the words are done as examples.

1. **affection**   *The father has great affection for the baby.*
2. **dispute**   _____
3. **gesture**   *The father is making an angry gesture with his hand.*
4. **grasp**   _____
5. **peril**   _____
6. **proceed**   *Cars and bicycles proceed on the busy street.*
7. **protest**   _____

8. reckless   _____

9. stationary   _____

10. vehicle   _____

CONTEXT CLUES

Here are ten passages. The lesson word that completes each passage has been left out. See if you can write the proper word in each blank. Look for helpful clues in the passage. If you are not absolutely sure, take a good guess.

1. The traffic was so heavy and snarled that not a car moved. All the cars were as _____ as though they had run out of gas.

2. Many animals show as much tenderness, care, and _____ for their babies as humans do.

3. _____ drivers do not take care about obeying safety regulations. They speed, pass red lights, and make illegal turns.

4. The motorcycle is a _____ with two wheels, while the automobile has four.

5. The finish was so close that a _____ arose about which runner won the race. The disagreement was finally settled by the photos.

6. Despite the warnings of a coming snowstorm, the travelers decided to _____ with their journey rather than call a halt to their plans.

7. The enthusiastic people watching the parade raised two fingers in the shape of a V, the well-known _____ of victory.

8. The people marched in the streets to _____ the super-highway planned for their now quiet village.

9. The flight was rough and frightening. Many of the passengers held on to their armrests in a _____ so tight that their knuckles turned white.

10. The great explorers of history knew they would face many an unknown _____, but their thirst for discovery was greater than their fear of danger.

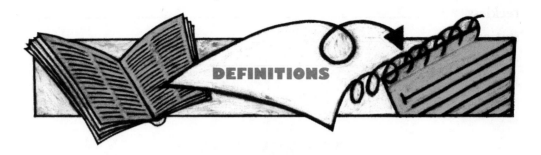

DEFINITIONS

Some words can be used as two or more parts of speech. The Table shows one part of speech and one meaning for each word. Study this information. After doing so, review your answers to Context Clues. Correct any errors.

Word	Part of Speech	Definition
affection	noun	a warm feeling; fondness; love
dispute	noun	an argument; quarrel; disagreement
gesture	noun	a movement or sign of any part of the body to express a meaning; signal; motion
grasp	noun	a firm hold with the hand; grip
peril	noun	a danger; risk
proceed	verb	to go; go on; continue
protest	verb	to speak against; argue; object to
reckless	adjective	careless; irresponsible
stationary	adjective	not moving; fixed in place
vehicle	noun	anything on wheels or runners for carrying people or things

THINKING

Show how well you can use the words as part of your thinking. In the space, write the lesson word that best answers the question.

1. People shrug their shoulders, shake a fist, and point a finger. Each of these is an example of what kind of action using the body?

   1. _____

2. If you are lost, you stop and get directions. After getting the directions, what do you then do?

   2. _____

3. What class of things do a parked car, a bronze statue in a park, a mountain, and a brick wall belong to that a raindrop does not?

   3. _____

4. What does a judge, an umpire, or a referee often try to settle? 4. _____

5. What emotion is usually felt by a parent for a child, a child for a pet dog, and a person for a close friend? 5. _____

6. What do fire fighters, police officers, and rescue squads often have to face? 6. _____

7. What is probably true of a driver who has had a lot of accidents? 7. _____

8. What use may a person's hand, an elephant's trunk, and a monkey's tail have in common? 8. _____

9. What are people who take part in picketing, demonstrations, and sit-ins usually trying to do? 9. _____

10. To what class of things do a sled, a cart, and a train belong that a house does not? 10. _____

GRAMMAR

A. Some words can be used as more than one part of speech. For example, some words can be used as either a noun or a verb. Four words of this kind are: **dispute, gesture, grasp, protest.** Here are examples.

dispute
- Noun: A **dispute** arose because of the government's failure to control pollution.
- Verb: Groups often **dispute** government policies about cleaning up the air.

gesture
- Noun: The gorilla made a threatening **gesture** at his trainer.
- Verb: Sports fans **gesture** their excitement by waving their arms.

grasp
- Noun: The gymnast's **grasp** on the bar was firm as she lifted herself above the floor.
- Verb: Monkeys **grasp** branches with their tails as well as their hands as they swing about.

protest
- Noun: The widespread **protest** against bus accidents finally brought about some action.
- Verb: Parents **protest** any move to cut back the school lunch program.

In the space provided, tell whether the word in heavy type is a noun or a verb.

1. The **dispute** between the drivers was settled by the police
   officer.   1. _____

2. Wrestlers often **grasp** their opponent by the leg to try for a
   fall.   2. _____

3. Soldiers **gesture** respect by saluting.   3. _____

4. Bus riders often **protest** a fare increase.   4. _____

5. Some people **dispute** the idea that vitamins are healthful.   5. _____

6. Shaking of the fist is a **gesture** that expresses anger.   6. _____

7. With a firm **grasp** on the ax handle, the log splitter swung
   at the wood.   7. _____

8. There was widespread **protest** in the town when the own-
   ers said they were going to close the steel mill.   8. _____

B. Nouns have two main forms: **singular** (*one*) and **plural** (*more than one*).
Most nouns form the plural by adding an s to the singular form.

SINGULAR (*one*)   **PLURAL** (*more than one*)
dispute   disputes

Write the plural of each noun below.

SINGULAR   **PLURAL**
gesture   _____
grasp   _____
protest   _____

C. Verbs have many different forms. Verbs have different forms for the three simple tenses: **present, past,** and **future.**

PRESENT	PAST	FUTURE
You dispute	You disputed	You will dispute
You gesture	You gestured	You will gesture
You grasp	You grasped	You will grasp
You protest	You protested	You will protest

Notice that the past tense is usually formed by adding **ed** or **d** to the present tense. (If the present ends in **e,** just add **d:** dispute + **d** = disput**ed.**)

For the future tense, use **will** before the present.

Write the form of the verb called for in each sentence below.

1. **dispute** (*future*)

   It seems sure that at the meeting next week, many people _____ the idea to build a new highway.

2. **gesture** (*past*)

   At the meeting yesterday, the majority _____ their approval by raising their hands.

3. **protest** (*present*)

   Fans often _____ the umpire's decision by booing.

4. **grasp** (*past*)

   The dog _____ the stick firmly in his jaws and brought it to us.

D. In the third person singular of the present tense, most verbs add an s.

PRESENT TENSE

First and second person singular	*Third person singular*
I dispute You dispute	He, She, or The boy disputes
I gesture You gesture	He, She, or The girl gestures
I grasp You grasp	He, She, or The man grasps
I protest You protest	He, She, or The woman protests

Write the third person singular form of the verb in each sentence.

1. **dispute**

   The only law that nobody _____ is the law of gravity.

2. **gesture**

   My dog _____ his happiness by wagging his tail.

3. **grasp**

   For a firm hold, a quarterback _____ the football by the seam.

4. **protest**

   The baby _____ with a loud cry whenever his bottle is taken away.

E. The part of speech (use in a sentence) of some words can be changed by adding a new ending (called a *suffix*). A few often-used suffixes are *ate, ly, ous,* and *able.*

affection	+ ate	=	affectionate
affectionate	+ ly	=	affectionately
peril	+ ous	=	perilous
perilous	+ ly	=	perilously
reckless	+ ly	=	recklessly
dispute − e	+ able	=	disputable

Change each numbered word to a different part of speech, if needed, so that it makes sense in the sentence. You will find the word forms you need in the examples above.

1. **affection**   The child was by nature warm and _____ toward everyone.

2. **peril**   The journey of Columbus was a _____ one.

3. **reckless**   The swimmer _____ ignored the dangerous tides and giant waves, and swam far out.

4. **peril**   The car was _____ close to the edge of the cliff.

5. **affection**   The baby _____ hugged his teddy bear.

6. **dispute**   The loud _____ could be heard in the corridor.

7. **peril**   The canoeists now faced the _____ of the rapids.

8. **dispute**   Many thought the jury's decision was quite _____.

9. **reckless**   A _____ driver is a peril to everyone.

10. **affection**   Some people are _____ while others are cold and distant.

In 8, did you subtract the **e** from **dispute** before adding the suffix?

WORDLORE

Synonyms

Words with the same or similar meanings are *synonyms*. For example, **little** and **small** are synonyms.

Here are five words from the list. They are printed in capital letters. Following each capitalized word is a group of four words. Three of these four are synonyms or near-synonyms of the capitalized word. Find these three synonyms and write them in the spaces provided. Then choose one of the three synonyms. Use that synonym correctly in a sentence of your own about yourself or someone you know.

1. STATIONARY

   fixed, hollow, still, unmoving

   Synonyms   1. _____   2. _____   3. _____

   Sentence _____

2. RECKLESS

   careless, happy, irresponsible, rash

   Synonyms   1. _____   2. _____   3. _____

   Sentence _____

3. DISPUTE

   argument, disagreement, error, quarrel

   Synonyms   1. _____   2. _____   3. _____

   Sentence _____

4. GRASP

   clasp, grip, hold, promise

   Synonyms   1. _____   2. _____   3. _____

   Sentence _____

5. PERIL

     danger, risk, jeopardy, plan

Synonyms 1. _____   2. _____   3. _____

Sentence _____

READING COMPREHENSION

Here is a reading passage that contains some of the lesson words. Read the passage. Then answer the questions that follow it.

The mountain climbers stopped to rest on a sheltered ledge. Suddenly, a fierce storm struck. A **dispute** arose. Should the group **proceed** or remain on the ledge until the storm has passed? Tempers grew short. With an angry **gesture** of his fist, one climber insisted they should go. Most of the others knew that there would be great **peril** in climbing during the storm. They began to **protest** against continuing.

Finally, the majority decided against **reckless** action. They remained **stationary** on the sheltered ledge. The storm ended as suddenly as it had struck. Then, with a firm **grasp** on ropes and ice axes, they once again began the climb to the peak.

1. When did a dispute arise? _____

_____

2. What was the dispute about? _____

_____

3. How did one climber show his anger? _____

_____

4. Why did the others disagree? _____

_____

5. What was the final decision? _____

_____

6. How did the incident work out? _____

_____

WRITING

Choose one of the following topics. Write a short paragraph on it. Try to use at least three of the lesson words or forms of them in your paragraph.

> A Family Disagreement
> Driving
> Beware, Danger!
> An Act of Kindness

_____

_____

_____

_____

_____

_____

_____

_____

See how many of the lesson words or forms of them you can find in newspapers, magazines, books, and other printed matter. If you find a word in newspapers or magazines that are ready to be thrown away, clip out the article or paragraph in which the word occurs. If you find any of the words in a book, copy the sentence in which the word appears. Then make a note of the title and author of the book. Your teacher will tell you when to bring your collection to class.

LESSON 2

LOOK AT THE PICTURE

What Did You See?

1. What is the work of the people who live here?

   _____

2. What are the two kinds of land that you can see?

   _____

   _____

3. What time of year is it?

   _____

4. In which building do the people probably live?

_____

5. What may some of the other buildings be for?

_____

_____

_____

6. Look at the roads. Do you see any traffic? What does this tell you?

_____

_____

_____

7. Where do you think this picture was taken from?

_____

PRONUNCIATION

Here are ten lesson words suggested by the picture. With the help of your teacher, pronounce each word.

agriculture   (ag′ rə kul′ chər)
contrast   (kon′ trast)
cultivate   (kul′ tə vāt)
drought   (drout)
fertile   (fėr′ tl)
foliage   (fō′ lē ij)
isolation   (ī′ sə lā′ shən)
panorama   (pan′ ə ram′ ə)
toil   (toil)
tranquil   (trang′ kwəl)

SPELLING

Be sure you know how to spell each word. Here are the words given in sentences. Letters are missing from each word. First put the missing letters where they belong. Then write each complete word in the space.

1. Our country is rich in farmlands. The products of our AGR__CUL__ __ __ __ include corn, wheat, vegetables, and fruit.

1. _____

2. There is a sharp CON __ __ __ST between the dry deserts of the Southwest and the green mountains and valleys of the North-west.

2. _____

3. Every farmer has to C__LT__V__ __ __ the land by plowing and fertilizing.

3. _____

4. When a DRO__ __ __T strikes, many crops are ruined by the lack of water.

4. _____

5. The farmlands of Iowa, Illinois, and Ne-braska are F__RT__LE. They easily grow vast crops to feed the nation.

5. _____

6. In the summer the trees were covered with green leaves. In the fall, this FOL__ __GE turned red and gold.

6. _____

7. The first pioneer families sometimes lived in I__ __LATION. There were no other people for hundreds of miles around.

7. _____

8. From the top of the mountain, they could see a vast PAN__R__MA of mountains, val-leys, forests, and rivers. They could see for many miles around into the land of three dif-ferent states.

8. _____

9. It took a lot of hard TO__L to build the railroads across the country. This labor was performed by workers who came from many different countries.

9. _____

10. The lake was calm and TRANQ__ __ __. Its surface was as smooth as a mirror. The wil-lows, unmoving in the still air, added to the peacefulness of the scene.

10. _____

How Do These Words Go With the Picture?

How well can you see the connection between each word and the picture? For as many words as you can, explain briefly how the word goes with the pic-ture. To help you, two of the words are done as examples.

1. **agriculture** — *The valley land is used for agriculture.*

2. **contrast** — *There is a contrast between the cleared land of the valley and the hills covered with trees.*

3. **cultivate** — _____

4. **drought** — _____

5. **fertile** — _____

6. foliage   _____

7. isolation   _____

8. panorama   _____

9. toil   _____

10. tranquil   _____

CONTEXT CLUES

Here are ten passages. The lesson word that completes each passage has been left out. See if you can write the proper word in each blank. Look for helpful clues in the passage. If you are not absolutely sure, take a good guess.

1. Industry produces cars, computers, and cement. _____ produces the food necessary to keep us alive.

2. Farmers have to _____ the soil. They have to remove stones and rocks, plow the soil, enrich the soil, and keep out weeds.

3. In his life of hard _____, the farmer had used his hands and the muscles of his back and legs. Now, he was worn out by the years of labor.

4. There had been no rain for months. This severe _____ had caused the lakes and rivers to dry up.

5. On the island, the weather was always clear and pleasant. The palm trees and clear, green sea provided a beautiful setting. The visitors spent the days in relaxation and peace. It was a _____ life.

6. The differences between the two men were noticed by everybody. One was short, stocky, well-dressed, and always smiling. The other was tall, thin as a rail, shabbily dressed, and sad-looking. This _____ was made greater by the talkativeness of the first and the silence of the second.

7. From the plane, the passengers could see the entire city with its closely packed buildings and its streets jammed with traffic. They could see the smokestacks of factories, the busy river that ran through the middle of the city, and the scores of small houses in the outlying districts. It was a _____ visible only from that great height.

8. In the forest the _____ was dense on the trees. The leaves formed a ceiling which very little sunlight could get through.

9. The hermit had lived in _____ in his cabin for years. He had had no contact with other human beings for all that time.

10. Irrigation canals carried water into what had once been dry land on which nothing could be grown. Now, the land was rich and _____, producing fruit, cotton, and vegetables.

DEFINITIONS

Most words have several meanings. Some words can be used as two or more parts of speech. The Table shows one part of speech and one meaning for each word. Study this information. After doing so, review your answers to Context Clues. Correct any errors.

Word	Part of Speech	Definition
agriculture	noun	farming; the science and art of producing crops and raising livestock
contrast	noun	a sharp difference between things or people being compared
cultivate	verb	to prepare and improve land for growing crops
drought	noun	the absence of rainfall or snow for a long time; a dry spell
fertile	adjective	able to produce richly
foliage	noun	the leaves of a plant or tree
isolation	noun	being alone; a separation from others
panorama	noun	an unlimited or wide view
toil	noun	hard, tiring work or labor
tranquil	adjective	peaceful, calm

THINKING

Sentence Sense

In each of the following sentences, the word in heavy type does not make good sense. Write a lesson word that will make the sentence sensible. Use the spaces to the right.

1. Years of backbreaking **rest** in the coal mines showed in his stooped shoulders and crippled hands.

1. _____

2. As a result of the long **rainfall**, the once-rich soil was turned to dry, useless dust.

2. _____

3. The tribe were a **warlike** people, always at peace with their neighbors.

3. _____

4. The **likeness** between the two towns was emphasized by the differences in the size of their police forces and the conditions of their streets.

4. _____

5. She was a woman who preferred **socializing**, and she always tried to avoid meeting other people.

5. _____

Word Quiz

Show how well you can use the words as part of your thinking. Answer each question by writing one of the words from the list.

1. In the spring, a gardener gets out the pitchfork, the spade, the hoe, and the rake. What is she getting ready to do to the soil in the garden?

1. _____

2. What do you usually need to be high on a hill or in a plane to see?

2. _____

3. There are many insect pests that eat up everything green. What will be missing from the trees after an attack by such insects?

3. _____

4. In a certain country, the people depend almost entirely for their food on what they can catch in the sea. What is the land probably not suited for in this country?

4. _____

5. Leonardo da Vinci was a great painter, scientist, and poet. What word can be used to describe his rich kind of mind?

5. _____

GRAMMAR

A. You know that some words can be used as either nouns or verbs. You know that nouns have two main forms—singular and plural. You know that verbs have many different forms. Two words that can be used as either a verb or a noun are **contrast** and **toil**.

Here are ten sentences. Tell whether the word in heavy type is a noun or a verb.

1. Many **contrasts** can be made between city life and country life.

2. Working in the mines is a life of hard **toil**.

3. No matter how hard she **toiled**, the work was never done.

4. The size of my dog **contrasts** sharply with the size of my friend's dog.

5. With the building of the new highway, the noise of traffic **contrasted** with the quiet streets of the old days.

6. The tall buildings and crowded streets of the city **contrast** with the peaceful hills and valleys of the country.

7. She **toils** in her garden mainly in the spring and autumn.

8. The **toils** of Hercules are told in the old myths.

9. There is often a noticeable **contrast** between what politicians say and what they do.

10. Construction workers often **toil** many floors above street level.

1. _____

2. _____

3. _____

4. _____

5. _____

6. _____

7. _____

8. _____

9. _____

10. _____

B. Look at the following pair of words.

VERB	NOUN
imitate	imitation

Many verbs end in **ate**. Such verbs can sometimes be changed to a noun by dropping the final **e** and adding the suffix **ion**.

Here are two more examples.

create	creation
rotate	rotation

The reverse is also true. Nouns ending in **ion** can be changed to a verb by dropping the **ion** and adding an **e**.

NOUN	VERB
punctuation	punctuate
fascination	fascinate

Now, use what you have learned to fill in the blanks.

NOUN	VERB
isolation	_____
_____	cultivate

C. In each of the following sentences, use the form of the word in parentheses that belongs in the sentence. The first is done for you as an example.

1. (*isolate, isolation*)   If you *isolate* yourself from others you may be lonely.

2. (*isolate, isolation*)   Hermits _____ themselves from society.

3. (*isolate, isolation*)   Hermits live in _____ , avoiding contact with others.

4. (*cultivate, cultivation*)   Each spring, gardeners _____ the soil.

5. (*Cultivate, Cultivation*)   _____ of the mind is a main purpose of education.

WORDLORE

Synonyms and Antonyms

As you know, many words have synonyms. Synonyms are words that mean the same or nearly the same as the given word.

Many words also have **antonyms**. Antonyms are words that mean the opposite or nearly the opposite of the given word. As an example, here are five pairs of antonyms.

hot - cold ● old - young ● rough - smooth ● big - little ● never - always

Here are five lesson words. Each is followed by two words. One of these two is a synonym of the lesson word. The other is an antonym. Tell which is which. In the space following each word, use S for synonym and A for antonym.

1. **drought**   rainfall _____   dryness _____

2. **fertile**   productive _____   barren _____

3. **isolation**	solitude _____	companionship _____
4. **toil**	rest _____	labor _____
5. **tranquil**	stormy _____	calm _____

Write two sentences of your own. In the first sentence use one of the words you have marked with an S. In the second, use one of the words you have marked with an A.

1. _____

_____

2. _____

_____

Prefixes for Antonyms

Many words begin with **prefixes**. The prefix in each of the following words is in heavy type.

>**sub**marine
>**re**consider
>**ad**mit
>**inter**rupt
>**pro**duce

Prefixes are beginning word parts. Prefixes help to form the meaning of a word.

Two important prefixes are **un** and **in**. The prefix **un** means *not*. The prefix **in** often means *not*. Therefore, antonyms of words can often be formed by adding the prefix **un** or the prefix **in**. Here are examples.

un		**in**	
Word	**Antonym**	**Word**	**Antonym**
happy	unhappy	active	inactive
able	unable	distinct	indistinct
broken	unbroken	direct	indirect
fair	unfair	complete	incomplete

Use the prefix **un** to form antonyms of the following words.

Word	**Antonym**	**Word**	**Antonym**
true	_____	lit	_____
healthy	_____	kind	_____
hurt	_____		

Use the prefix **in** to form antonyms of the following words.

Word	Antonym	Word	Antonym
correct	_____	secure	_____
curable	_____	human	_____
definite	_____		

Write two sentences about something in the news. In each sentence, use one of the antonyms you have formed.

1. _____

_____

2. _____

_____

READING COMPREHENSION

Here is a reading passage that contains some of the lesson words. Read the passage. Then answer the questions that follow it.

Early pioneers settled in South Dakota to farm the land. Enormous **toil** was required to **cultivate** the grasslands of the plains. All this labor was often wasted when crops were lost in long periods of **drought.** Sometimes, crops were lost when hordes of locusts or grasshoppers devoured all the **foliage.** The families of these settlers lived in sod huts in almost total **isolation** from other people. It was a hard and lonely life.

Today, there is a sharp **contrast.** The soil is rich and **fertile,** and South Dakota is a leader in **agriculture.** With modern methods, farmers have some protection against **drought** and insect pests. Life is far more **tranquil** and rewarding for the farmers.

1. Why did some early pioneers settle in South Dakota? _____

   _____

2. What kind of land did they have to cultivate? _____

3. Name two problems these farmers had in raising crops. _____

   _____

4. Why was their life often lonely? _____

   _____

5. Name two ways in which the life of South Dakota farmers is different today from life in the early days. _____

   _____

   _____

WRITING

The title of your short paragraph is **CONTRAST**. In your paragraph, tell about two or three important differences between two people you know well or two places you know well.

_____

_____

_____

_____

_____

ASSIGNMENT

See how many of the lesson words or forms of them you can find in newspapers, magazines, books, and other printed matter. If you find a word in newspapers or magazines that are ready to be thrown away, clip out the article or paragraph in which the word occurs. If you find any of the words in a book, copy the sentence in which the word appears. Then make a note of the title and author of the book. Your teacher will tell you when to bring your collection to class.

LESSON 3

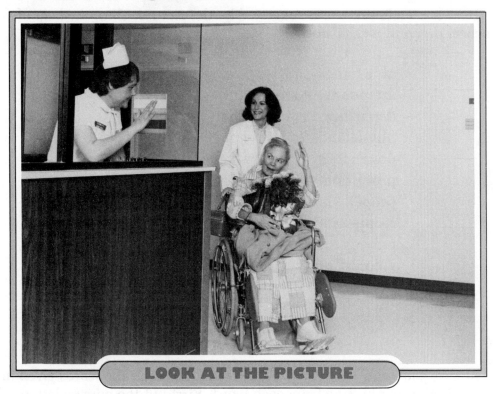

LOOK AT THE PICTURE

What Did You See?

1. Where is this scene taking place?

_____

2. Who are the three people?

_____

_____

_____

3. How do the three people feel? Why?

_____

_____

4. What vehicle do you see?

_____

5. What does one woman have in her lap?

_____

PRONUNCIATION

Here are ten lesson words suggested by the picture. With the help of your teacher, pronounce each word.

aide   (ād)
attendant   (ə ten′ dənt)
departure   (di pär′ chər)
physician   (fə zish′ ən)
possessions   (pə zesh′ ənz)
profession   (prə fesh′ ən)
propel   (prə pel′)
recuperate   (ri kü′ pə rāt′)
remedy   (rem′ ə dē)
volunteer   (vol′ ən tir′)

SPELLING

Be sure you know how to spell each word. Here are the words given in sentences. Letters are missing from each word. First put the missing letters where they belong. Then write each complete word in the space.

1. The elderly couple were assisted by a home __IDE who did some shopping and cooking for them.   1. _____

2. An A__ __END__NT was on duty to give visitors to the museum any information they needed.   2. _____

3. The D__PAR__ __RE of the great ship from the dock was accompanied by whistles and toots from all the boats in the harbor.   3. _____

4. The P__ __SIC__AN suggested regular exercise and a well-balanced diet but did not prescribe any medicine.   4. _____

5. The refugees fled hastily, leaving all their PO_ _ _E_ _ _IONS behind except the clothes on their backs.

5. _____

6. Before you can enter the legal PROFE_ _ _ _ON, you need to complete law school and pass the bar examination given by the state.

6. _____

7. We felt a bumping of the wheels as the jet engines began to PROP_ _ _ the plane down the runway.

7. _____

8. The clean mountain air and my daily walk along the edge of the lake helped me to RE_ _ _ _ERATE rapidly, and in a week I was my old self again.

8. _____

9. There is no known RE_ _ _DY for the common cold, which simply has to cure itself.

9. _____

10. Though every fire fighter in the town was a VOL_ _NT_ _ _R, they were as good as any paid force of fire fighters.

10. _____

How Do These Words Go With the Picture?

How well can you see the connection between each word and the picture? For as many words as you can, explain briefly how each word goes with the picture.

1. **aide** _____

2. **attendant** _____

3. **departure** _____

4. **physician** _____

5. **possessions** _____

6. **profession** _____

7. **propel** _____

8. **recuperate** _____

9. **remedy** _____

10. **volunteer** _____

CONTEXT CLUES

Here are ten passages. The lesson word that completes each passage has been left out. See if you can write the proper word in each blank. Look for helpful clues in the passage. If you are not absolutely sure, take a good guess.

1. The _____ in the locker room was paid to look after the equipment, help the players, and keep the room in shipshape order.

2. Snakes don't have feet on which to move forward. Instead they _____ themselves along the ground by movements of their bodies.

3. I wonder whether this _____ isn't worse than the illness it is supposed to cure. It makes my head dizzy and my throat dry.

4. She enjoys her work as a _____ worker in the community center. Her reward is not money but the satisfaction of helping others.

5. The _____ was constantly at the side of the general. The general gave the orders and the assistant saw that they were carried out.

6. The _____ of the train from the station was delayed. It did not leave until 9:30 A.M.

7. The doctor told the patient that it would take only a week to _____ from the operation. Then she would be as healthy as ever.

8. While still in elementary school, he decided that he wanted to enter the teaching _____ . He looked forward to the time when he would enter college and begin the training for his chosen career.

9. Everything they owned was loaded into the moving van. Without these _____ , the home they had lived in for so many years seemed a strange place.

10. The _____ wore a white coat and had a stethoscope hanging from his neck. These seem to be the badges of doctors everywhere.

Most words have several meanings. Some words can be used as two or more parts of speech. The Table shows one part of speech and one meaning for each word. Study this information. After doing so, review your answers to Context Clues. Correct any errors.

Word	Part of Speech	Definition
aide	noun	a helper; assistant
attendant	noun	a person who serves or looks after things
departure	noun	leaving; going away
physician	noun	a medical doctor
possessions	noun	things owned by a person
profession	noun	an occupation requiring special and advanced training (doctor, nurse, lawyer, engineer, teacher)
propel	verb	to push or push forward
recuperate	verb	to become well again after an illness or injury
remedy	noun	any medicine or treatment that cures
volunteer	noun	a person who does some work of his or her own free will, sometimes without pay

THINKING

Odd Word Out

One of the lesson words is shown in capital letters. It is followed by four other words or phrases. Three of these four belong closely with the capitalized word. One does not. Cross out the "stranger."

1. PHYSICIAN: stethoscope   violin   medicine   hospital
2. REMEDY: aspirin   heating pad   rest   envelope
3. DEPARTURE: stove   travel   good-bye   destination
4. POSSESSIONS: clothing   furniture   bicycle   air
5. PROPEL: sleep   motion   push   wheels

Below are five of the lesson words. Four of these words are in the class of things "having something to do with work." One is not. Cross out the "stranger."

aide   attendant   profession   recuperate   volunteer

GRAMMAR

Form new words by following the directions. Then write the new words in the sentences.

1. The word **possessions** is a plural noun. Write the singular form. _____

   Thoreau lived a simple life with hardly a _____.

2. The word **physician** is a singular noun. Write the plural form. _____

   Bruce visited many _____ before he found one who discovered he was allergic to milk.

3. Write the plural form of the noun **profession**. _____

   Many new _____ have come into being in this age of technology.

4. Change the verb **recuperate** to a noun. _____

   Her _____ from the operation took several weeks.

5. Change the noun **possession** to a verb by dropping the final **ion**. _____

   Some people _____ their own library of good books.

6. Change **departure** to a verb by dropping the final **ure**. _____

   When is the next train scheduled to _____?

7. Change **attendant** to a verb by dropping the final **ant**. _____

   Lisa was asked to _____ to the cleaning of the chalkboards.

8. Change **remedy** to an adjective. Change the y to an **i** and add **al**. _____

   The _____ reading class meets three times a week.

   Now answer the following questions about words and how they are used.

9. The word **remedy** can be a noun or a verb. Which is it in this sentence?

   "I will remedy your sore throat," said the doctor. _____

10. The word **volunteer** can be a noun or a verb. Which is it in this sentence?

    Why do you always volunteer to wash the dishes? _____

WORDLORE

Rhymes

Have a little fun with rhymes. Choose a lesson word to complete each of the following rhymes.

1. I'd like to be making a simple confession.

   My teeth hate the work of the dental _____ .

2. The room is a mess and the bed is unmade.

   It will all be repaired by the new nurse's _____ .

3. When they lose a game, they don't feel great.

   If they win next week, they'll _____ .

4. The student had a noble ambition.

   She wanted to be a children's _____ .

5. The cat struts in, a proud little marcher.

   Takes one look around and makes his _____ .

Anagrams

One word can be made into another by rearranging the letters. Here are some examples:

now — won — own

rat — tar — art

This "game" is called **anagrams**.

Try these:

1. Rearrange the letters of AIDE to form a word meaning "a thought."   1. _____

2. Add an S to the letters in AIDE and rearrange the letters to form a word meaning "apart" or "on the side."   2. _____

3. Add an L to the word you formed in (2) and rearrange the letters to form a word meaning "moved across the water in a boat or ship."   3. _____

4. Rearrange the letters of the word in (3) to form a word meaning "many women."   4. _____

5. Add a B to the word in (4) and rearrange the letters to form a word meaning "to make unfit for use."   5. _____

6. Subtract an L from the word in (5) and rearrange the letters to form a word meaning "of one opinion" or "prejudiced."   6. _____

READING COMPREHENSION

On the next page is a reading passage that contains some of the lesson words. Read the passage. Then answer the questions that follow it.

My little brother had to have his tonsils out. He took with him to the hospital his favorite **possessions,** the teddy bear and the security blanket. When we arrived, an **attendant** asked a lot of questions and then directed us to the room. There, a nurse's **aide** helped him to get settled. She was followed by a **volunteer** worker who allowed him to select toys, games, and books from her cart. Finally, the **physician** came into the room. He joked around with my brother to cheer him up. He told my brother that the operation would be the best **remedy** for the sore throats he was always having. The doctor also said that my brother would get a lot of ice cream after the operation.

Three days later, my little brother was ready for the **departure** home. There, he found a present, a shiny new tricycle. It took him but a few days to **recuperate** fully and become himself once more. We watched him **propel** himself on the trike like a madman all around the house. Soon he was getting in everybody's hair more than ever. His first experience with the medical **profession** was a success!

1. What possessions did the little brother bring with him to the hospital?

_____

2. Who asked a lot of questions? What might two of these questions have been?

_____

_____

_____

3. Who helped the little brother get settled in the room?

_____

_____

4. What kind of worker gave him toys, games, and books? On what kind of vehicle did she propel these items around the hospital?

_____

_____

5. What was the operation meant to remedy?

_____

6. After his departure from the hospital, what did the little brother find at home?

_____

_____

7. What happened after the little brother recuperated fully?

_____

_____

WRITING

Write a short paragraph about a time when someone you know was sick. Try to use at least three of the lesson words or forms of them in your paragraph.

_____

_____

_____

_____

_____

_____

_____

_____

See how many of the lesson words or forms of them you can find in newspapers, magazines, books, and other printed matter. If you find a word in newspapers or magazines that are ready to be thrown away, clip out the article or paragraph in which the word occurs. If you find any of the words in a book, copy the sentence in which the word appears. Then make a note of the title and author of the book. Your teacher will tell you when to bring your collection to class.

LESSON 4

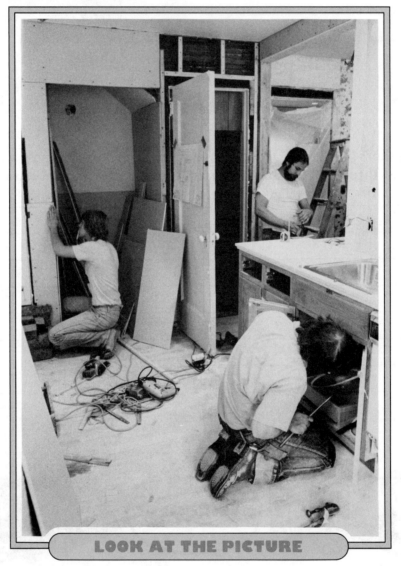

LOOK AT THE PICTURE

What Did You See?

1. What are the three people doing?

_____

_____

2. Each of the three may do a different kind of work. If so, what is probably the work of the man in the front?

_____

3. What is probably the work of the man to the left?

_____

4. What is probably the work of the man standing to the right?

_____

5. Why is there a jumble of wires on the floor?

_____

_____

6. Would someone looking at this picture feel that these are good, reliable workmen or not? Why do you think so?

_____

_____

PRONUNCIATION

Here are ten lesson words suggested by the picture. With the help of your teacher, pronounce each word.

concentrate   (kon′ sən trāt)
construction   (kən struk′ shən)
craft   (kraft)
dwelling   (dwel′ ing)
extension   (ek sten′ shən)
function   (fungk′ shən)
implement   (im′ plə mənt)
schedule   (skej′ ül)
skillful   (skil′ fəl)
teamwork   (tēm′ wėrk′)

SPELLING

Be sure you know how to spell each word. On the next page are the words given in sentences. Letters are missing from each word. First put the missing letters where they belong. Then write each complete word in the space.

1. Persons who CON__ __ __TRATE on their work instead of letting their minds wander are less likely to make mistakes.

2. Steel and concrete were the main materials used in the CONSTRU__ __ __ __N of the skyscraper to make sure that it was built to last.

3. The Navajos are outstanding in the C__ __FT of rug weaving and the Hopis are known for the beautiful baskets they make so well.

4. The family was very happy in their new home, a simple country D__E__ __ __NG surrounded by green fields and tall trees.

5. The wire of the lamp was not long enough to reach the outlet, so they had to add an EXT__N__ __ __N to get the lamp plugged in.

6. The FUN__ __ __ __N of a saw is to cut wood, while a plane is used to smooth the wood.

7. Scissors are an important IMP__ __M__NT around the house. The screwdriver is another useful tool.

8. The busy homemaker had every moment of her day carefully planned, and she stuck to her S__ __EDULE without fail.

9. The boy's hobby was photography, and he was so SKI__ __FU__ that every picture he took was perfect.

10. In sailing a boat, T__AM__ORK among the crew is necessary. If the crew doesn't work together, everything will go wrong.

1. _____

2. _____

3. _____

4. _____

5. _____

6. _____

7. _____

8. _____

9. _____

10._____

How Do These Words Go With the Picture?

How well can you see the connection between each word and the picture? For as many words as you can, explain briefly how each word goes with the picture.

1. **concentrate** _____

2. **construction** _____

3. **craft** _____

4. dwelling   _____

5. extension   _____

6. function   _____

7. implement   _____

8. schedule   _____

9. skillful   _____

10. teamwork   _____

CONTEXT CLUES

Here are ten passages. The lesson word that completes each passage has been left out. See if you can write the proper word in each blank. Look for helpful clues in the passage. If you are not absolutely sure, take a good guess.

1. Bill studied the train _____ carefully. He saw that an express for Chicago was set to leave at 4:00 P.M.

2. Grandmother was coming to live with the family. Since the house was rather small, they decided to add an _____ so that she could have her own room.

3. When Amelia was reading a book, she would _____ so hard that she didn't pay attention to anything else going on around her.

4. My Mom is a _____ carpenter. She is also very good at electrical work and she is an expert mechanic. Therefore, she does most of the repair work around the house herself.

5. Long ago the typical _____ was a farmhouse or cabin. Now, most people make their homes in cities or towns.

6. Whenever a new building is put up, the noises and dust of the

_____ bother everybody around.

7. The needle is the main tool in sewing. The loom is the important

_____ of the weaver.

8. Axes have many uses. One common _____ of the axe is to chop firewood.

9. The _____ of the carpenter is a special skill that is important to everyday living. The special ability of the glassblower, however, is used mainly to create beautiful objects.

10. In a game like football, it can't be every man for himself. _____ is essential.

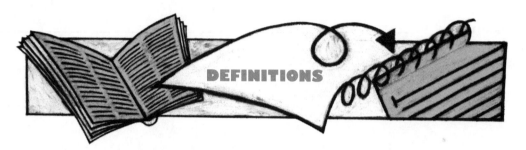

Most words have several meanings. Some words can be used as two or more parts of speech. The Table shows one part of speech and one meaning for each word. Study this information. After doing so, review your answers to Context Clues. Correct any errors.

Word	Part of Speech	Definition
concentrate	verb	to pay close attention; focus the mind on
construction	noun	the act of building; act of putting together
craft	noun	a trade or kind of work requiring special skill or ability
dwelling	noun	the place in which one lives; house; residence
extension	noun	something added, such as a room or a length of wire
function	noun	a use or purpose
implement	noun	a tool; device; utensil
schedule	noun	the times fixed for doing things; program
skillful	adjective	having a special ability; being expert
teamwork	noun	the acting together of two or more people; cooperation

THINKING

Sentence Sense

In each of the following sentences, one word does not make good sense. Cross it out and write a lesson word that will make the sentence sensible. Use the spaces to the right.

1. The carpenter was very clumsy, and we watched in admiration as he put together the new kitchen cabinets.

   1. _____

2. A skyscraper was under water, with steelworkers, riveters, plumbers, and electricians all busy in putting up the new building.

   2. _____

3. The purpose of a radiator is to provide heat while the cost of a lamp is to give light.

   3. _____

4. The mattress we added to our garden hose made it possible to reach all the flower beds that we could not reach before we attached the extra length.

   4. _____

5. If you stand especially on the first chapter, you will easily understand all the following chapters.

   5. _____

Matching

In the space next to each word in Column I, write the word from Column II that best goes with it.

		I	II
_____	1.	craft	hammer
_____	2.	dwelling	timetable
_____	3.	implement	needlework
_____	4.	schedule	basketball
_____	5.	teamwork	cottage

GRAMMAR

A. The words **schedule** and **function** can be either a noun or a verb. Tell whether the word in heavy type in the following sentences is a noun or a verb.

1. The boss **scheduled** a meeting for ten o'clock.

   1. _____

2. What is the **function** of a battery?

   2. _____

3. Gears can have several different **functions**.

   3. _____

4. This valve **functions** to shut off the water if the pressure gets too high.

   4. _____

5. In ancient times, horses **functioned** as the main means of transportation.

   5. _____

6. The **schedules** of games for the next two years are prepared.

   6. _____

7. The teacher **schedules** a test for the last day of each week.　　7. _____

8. Do you have the **schedule** of T.V. programs for tonight?　　8. _____

9. Try to **schedule** the meeting for tomorrow.　　9. _____

10. Oils and greases **function** to reduce friction.　　10. _____

B. Form new words by following the directions. Then write the new words in the sentences.

1. Change **skillful** to a noun by dropping the suffix **ful**. _____

    Though he was small for a football player, his _____ at passing made him a great quarterback.

2. Change **dwelling** to a verb by dropping the suffix **ing**. _____

    Kings and nobles used to _____ in castles, while peasants lived in huts.

3. Change **construction** to a verb by dropping the suffix **ion**. _____

    The town decided to _____ a new school.

4. Change **extension** to a verb by dropping the suffix **ion** and changing the final s to a **d**. _____

    Lean forward and _____ your arms as far as you can. See if you can touch your toes without bending your knees.

5. Change **concentration** to a verb by dropping the suffix **ion** and adding a final **e**.

    _____

    Most students have to _____ hard when writing a composition.

WORDLORE

Synonyms and Antonyms

Each lesson word below is followed by three words. One of these three words is either a synonym or an antonym of the lesson word. Write the synonym or antonym in the space provided. Tell which it is by using S for synonym and A for antonym.

1. CRAFT: skill, button, truth　　_____ _____

2. DWELLING: furniture, distance, residence　　_____ _____

3. CONSTRUCTION: space, destruction, part _____ _____

4. TEAMWORK: selfishness, labor, laziness _____ _____

5. FUNCTION: experiment, wish, use _____ _____

The Dictionary

Many people may think that a single word is a simple thing. You know better. It is a sound (when we say it) and a spelling (when we write it). It may be used as one or more parts of speech in a sentence and may have many different forms and meanings. It may have synonyms and antonyms. It has a history.

The best place to find much of the rich information about a word is a good dictionary.

Below is the entry for the word **craft**. Read the entry. Then answer the questions that follow.

> **craft** (kraft), *n.* **1** special skill: *The potter shaped the clay into a pitcher with great craft.* **2** trade or work requiring special skill. **3** members of a trade requiring special skill: *Carpenters belong to a craft.* **4** skill in deceiving others; slyness; trickiness: *By craft the gambler tricked them out of all their money.* **5** boats, ships, or aircraft. **6** a boat, ship, or aircraft. —*v.t.* work, make, or finish with skill or art: *woodwork crafted by expert cabinetmakers.* [Old English *cræft*]

1. How many syllables does **craft** have? _____

2. **Craft** can be a noun or a verb. What abbreviation tells you that it can be a noun?

   _____

   _____

3. One meaning of **craft** is "special skill." What sentence is given to illustrate this meaning? _____

   _____

4. What are two other totally different meanings that the noun **craft** can have?

   _____

   _____

Here is a reading passage that contains most of the lesson words. Read the passage. Then answer the questions that follow it.

It was an unusual **dwelling** on the side of the mountain. Years earlier it had been built by one man as a simple one-room log cabin. The chief **implement** used was an ax. Every few years, a new **extension** had been added on to the original building. Now, the main materials of the new **construction** were steel and glass. The newest addition to the residence, a large workshop, studio, and playroom, required **teamwork** among experts in many a **craft.** These **skillful** people had to work according to a carefully planned **schedule.** The **function** of the original log cabin was to serve as the summer vacation home of one person who wanted to get away from it all. Now it was the beautiful year-round home and workplace of a large family.

1. Where was the original dwelling?

   _____

2. What kind of dwelling was it?

   _____

3. What was the main implement used in building it?

   _____

4. What was done over the years?

   _____

5. What were the main materials of the new construction?

_____

6. What did the newest construction require?

_____

7. How did the function of the dwelling change?

_____

_____

WRITING

Write a short paragraph about the work done by someone you know. In your paragraph, try to use at least three of the lesson words or forms of them.

_____

_____

_____

_____

_____

_____

_____

_____

See how many of the lesson words or forms of them you can find in newspapers, magazines, books, and other printed matter. If you find a word in newspapers or magazines that are ready to be thrown away, clip out the article or paragraph in which the word occurs. If you find any of the words in a book, copy the sentence in which the word appears. Then make a note of the title and author of the book. Your teacher will tell you when to bring your collection to class.

REVIEW LESSONS 1-4

LOOK AT THE PICTURE

What Did You See?

1. What is happening?

   _____

   _____

2. What season is it?

   _____

3. Are the fire fighters working alone, or together as a team?

_____

_____

4. Name three pieces of equipment used by the fire fighters.

_____

_____

Here are the forty words you have learned so much about in Lessons 1-4. First, review the list by saying each word aloud. Then go on to the review exercises and refer to this list as you need to.

affection	agriculture	aide	concentrate
dispute	contrast	attendant	construction
gesture	cultivate	departure	craft
grasp	drought	physician	dwelling
peril	fertile	possessions	extension
proceed	foliage	profession	function
protest	isolation	propel	implement
reckless	panorama	recuperate	schedule
stationary	toil	remedy	skillful
vehicle	tranquil	volunteer	teamwork

How Do These Words Go With the Picture?

Here are three lesson words. Briefly explain the connection of each to the picture.

1. **grasp**   _____

2. **peril**   _____

3. **teamwork** _____

Now select from the review list five other lesson words that you feel are connected to the picture. Write each word and briefly explain the connection.

_____   _____

_____   _____

_____   _____

_____   _____

Ideas

You are given words suggesting a general idea. For each, select three lesson words that are closely connected with the idea. Write the words. Then choose one word and write it in a sentence of your own. The first has been done for you as an example.

1. WORK

   Words: _schedule_ _toil_ _craft_

   Sentence: _On Fridays, the doctor always has a_
   busy schedule.

2. FAMILY LIFE

   Words: _____ _____ _____

   Sentence: _____

   _____

3. NATURE

   Words: _____ _____ _____

   Sentence: _____

   _____

4. TRAVEL

   Words: _____ _____ _____

   Sentence: _____

   _____

Scrambled Words and Anagrams

Here are five lesson words with the letters scrambled. On line **a,** write the word with the letters in the correct order. On line **b,** follow the instructions for each word.

1. SPARG   a. _____

   Add *E* to the letters of your word and use
   those letters to form a new word meaning "a fruit
   that grows in bunches."   b. _____

2. RELIP   a. _____

   Add *P* to the letters of your word and use
   those letters to form a new word meaning "a tiny
   wave on the surface of water."   b. _____

3. ILTO   a. _____

    Add *P* to the letters of your word and use those letters to form a new word meaning "someone who drives a plane or a ship."   b. _____

4. FCTRA   a. _____

    Add *O* and *Y* to the letters of your word and use those letters to form a new word meaning "a place where things are manufactured."   b. _____

5. DEAI   a. _____

    Add *M* and *R* to the letters of your word to form a new word meaning "to have feelings of approval and respect for."   b. _____

GRAMMAR

A. Write the plurals of these nouns.

1. affection   _____

2. dispute   _____

3. peril   _____

4. volunteer   _____

5. drought   _____

Use any one of the words you have written in a sentence of your own.

_____

_____

B. Drop the endings to change these nouns to verbs. Then write the verbs in the sentences.

1. **construction**

    With a ruler and a compass you can easily _____ a right angle.

2. **attendant**

    When the home team is ahead, fans _____ the games in large numbers.

3. **isolation** (watch for the *e* ending!)

    In a hospital, doctors _____ patients with highly contagious diseases.

C. Add **d** or **ed** to these verbs to form the past tense.

1. dispute   _____

2. proceed   _____

3. concentrate   _____

4. schedule   _____

5. contrast   _____

Use any one of the words you have written in a sentence of your own.

_____

_____

D. Change these verbs to nouns. (Remember to drop the final *e* in forming the new word.) Then write the nouns in the sentences.

1. **cultivate**

    Thorough _____ breaks up the soil and allows new plants to take hold and grow.

2. **recuperate**

    Grandfather hurt his hip when he fell; his _____ was much more rapid than anyone expected.

3. **concentrate**

    Few games require as much intense _____ as chess.

The Dictionary

Here is the dictionary entry for **function.** Look it over. Answer the questions.

> **function** (fungk′ shən),*n.* 1 proper work; normal action or use; purpose: *The function of the stomach is to help digest food.* 2 duty or office; employment. 3 a formal public or social gathering for some purpose, such as a wedding. 4 in mathematics: **a** quantity whose value depends on, or varies with, the value given to one or more variable quantities: *The area of a circle is a function of its radius.* **b** a relationship between two sets such that each element in the first set is associated with exactly one element in the second set. 5 anything likened to a mathematical function. 6 (in grammar) the way in which a word or phrase is used in a sentence. —*v.i.* perform a function or one's functions; work; be used; act: *One of the older students can function as teacher.* [< Latin *functionem* < *fungi* perform]

1. The letter **n.** appears in the first line. What does this tell you?

   _____

2. What is the function of the stomach?

   _____

3. What special meaning does **function** have in grammar?

   _____

4. In what other school subject does **function** have a special meaning?

   _____

5. Give one word that tells what **function** means when it is used as a verb.

   _____

6. From what ancient language does **function** come?

   _____

READING

Fill-ins

Here are three reading passages. Five words are missing from each, as the numbered blanks show. After each passage is a list of seven words. From this list, choose the word that makes the best sense in each blank space.

A. A speeding car struck a woman and the driver of the (1) _____ raced away. The woman was rushed to a hospital. There a(n) (2) _____ immediately wheeled her into an examination room. A doctor came in. This (3) _____ examined her carefully. Luckily, the only damage he found were a couple of minor cuts easy to (4) _____ with medication and bandages. The doctor said the woman should just take a few hours' rest and then could (5) _____ home.

agriculture	physician
attendant	proceed
contrast	remedy
vehicle	

B. In the old days, families relied on themselves for their basic needs. The spinning wheel was a common device in the home. The (1) _____ of a spinning wheel was to make thread and yarn. Besides that tool, another home (2) _____ was the loom for weaving the thread into the cloth from which clothing was made. Many members of the family were likely to be (3) _____ with both these devices. Many homes had vegetable gardens which the family would (4) _____ for that part of their food supply. When special skills were required, every village had experts in some (5) _____ . The carpenter had the know-how to work on wood, the blacksmith on iron.

craft   function
cultivate   implement
drought   peril
skillful

C. It had not rained for months. The (1) _____ on the trees has lost its green. It was dry and brown. Everyone worried about the (2) _____ of forest fires. People in the area began to pack up their most precious (3) _____ and get ready to flee from the area. The authorities began to organize fire fighting brigades. They asked able-bodied citizens to (4) _____ for this work if the need should arise. Then, suddenly, heavy rains came. The rain lasted for days and the danger was over. The worry and excitement came to an end. All was normal and (5) _____ once again.

concentrate   peril
departure   possessions
foliage   tranquil
volunteer

TEST YOURSELF

From Column II select the best definition of each word in Column I. Write the letter for the definition in the space next to each word.

I   II

A

_____ 1. stationary   a. addition
_____ 2. extension   b. argument
_____ 3. proceed   c. movement of part of the body
_____ 4. gesture   d. unmoving
_____ 5. dispute   e. go on

B

_____ 1. schedule   a. being alone
_____ 2. concentrate   b. house
_____ 3. dwelling   c. program
_____ 4. isolation   d. argue; object to
_____ 5. protest   e. pay close attention

C

_____ 1. affection   a. sharp differences
_____ 2. grasp   b. get better
_____ 3. contrast   c. push forward
_____ 4. recuperate   d. fondness
_____ 5. propel   e. grip

D

_____ 1. fertile   a. peaceful
_____ 2. toil   b. act of leaving
_____ 3. profession   c. producing richly
_____ 4. tranquil   d. occupation requiring special training
_____ 5. departure   e. labor

LESSON 5

LOOK AT THE PICTURE

What Did You See?

1. In what kind of building is this scene probably taking place?

   _____

2. What implements are the people using?

   _____

3. What are they doing besides looking?

   _____

   _____

4. What subject are these people probably studying?

_____

5. Take a guess as to what is being seen.

_____

_____

PRONUNCIATION

Here are ten lesson words suggested by the picture. With the help of your teacher, pronounce each word.

adjust   (ə just′)
diligently   (dil′ ə jənt lē)
instrument   (in′ strə mənt)
investigate   (in ves′ tə gāt)
laboratory   (lab′ rə tôr′ ē)
microscope   (mī′ krə skōp)
observation   (ob′ zər vā′ shən)
peer   (pir)
record   (ri kôrd′)
scientific   (sī′ ən tif′ ik)

SPELLING

Be sure you know how to spell each word. Here are the words given in sentences. Letters are missing from each word. First put the missing letters where they belong. Then write each complete word in the space.

1. If the picture on your TV is too dark, you can A___ ___UST the proper knob to make it brighter.

   1. _____

2. Some people do their work DIL___ ___ ___NTLY while others are lazy and unreliable.

   2. _____

3. Dentists often use a pointed metal INS___ ___ ___M___NT to check the teeth for cavities.

   3. _____

4. When the explosion occurred, experts were called in to INVES___ ___ ___ ___TE the cause.

   4. _____

5. The new LAB __ __ __ TORY had all kinds of special equipment so that experts could perform experiments in gene-splicing.

5. _____

6. Bacteria cannot be seen by the naked eye, but a M__ __ __ __ SCOPE magnifies them many times so that they can be seen.

6. _____

7. The watchful eyes of the bridge inspectors saw dangerous cracks. Their trained powers of OBS__ __ V__ __ ION prevented a tragedy.

7. _____

8. The prices written on the tags were so small that shoppers had to P__ __ R closely before they could read the numbers.

8. _____

9. Every city has a special office whose duty is to R__ __ ORD births and deaths. It is important to put the facts in writing and keep them for many reasons.

9. _____

10. Many students are interested in the experiments and laws of such subjects as chemistry and biology. These students often go on to S__ __ __ NTIFIC careers.

10. _____

How Do These Words Go With the Picture?

How well can you see the connection between each word and the picture? For as many words as you can, explain briefly how the word goes with the picture.

1. **adjust**   _____

2. **diligently**   _____

3. **instrument**   _____

4. **investigate**   _____

5. **laboratory**   _____

6. **microscope**   _____

7. **observation**   _____

8. **peer**   _____

9. record _____

10. scientific _____

CONTEXT CLUES

Here are ten passages. The lesson word that completes each passage has been left out. See if you can write the proper word in each blank. Look for helpful clues in the passage. If you are not absolutely sure, take a good guess.

1. The large room had all kinds of equipment and implements. Students were busily at work performing experiments. It was a fine, modern school

   _____ .

2. Good newspapers _____ all the important events of the day on the first page. These written accounts are kept for later study by historians.

3. The music is too loud. Please _____ the volume knob so that the music is a bit softer.

4. The mayor appointed a committee to study the traffic problem. They would

   _____ ways to reduce traffic tie-ups.

5. She studied for the exam _____ two hours a day for a week. Her efforts were rewarded by an excellent grade on the test.

6. Look at this drop of pond water. It seems perfectly clear. Now look at the

   drop under a _____ . You can see that it is full of tiny living creatures.

7. Einstein was _____ . He accepted no idea or theory unless it could be proved by experiment.

8. Einstein was helped by new powerful telescopes. These telescopes made possible

   _____ of distant stars which could not be seen and watched before.

9. Underwater swimmers _____ through the glass of their masks trying to see the strange fish in the dark water.

10. The violin is a device for producing music by vibrating strings. The flute is a(n)

   _____ for producing music by a vibrating column of air.

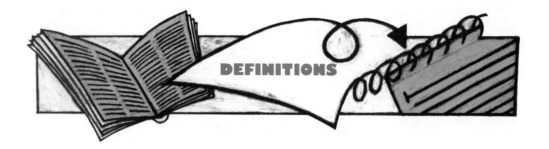

Most words have several meanings. Some words can be used as two or more parts of speech. The Table shows one part of speech and one meaning for each word. Study this information. After doing so, review your answers to Context Clues. Correct any errors.

Word	Part of Speech	Definition
adjust	verb	to change or rearrange something to make it more suitable
diligently	adverb	done in a hardworking, industrious manner
instrument	noun	a tool, implement, or device
investigate	verb	to look into thoroughly; examine carefully; study
laboratory	noun	a place where scientific work is done; a room with special equipment for scientific investigation
microscope	noun	an instrument consisting of a combination of lenses for magnifying things that are too small for the naked eye to see
observation	noun	the act of careful watching and studying
peer	verb	to look closely in order to see clearly
record	verb	to set down in writing to keep for future use
scientific	adjective	having to do with science or systems of knowledge based on observed facts and ideas tested by experiment

THINKING

Word Quiz

Show how well you can use the words as part of your thinking. In the space, write the lesson word that best answers the question.

1. What class of things do a microscope, a hammer, and a tire pressure gauge belong to that a sandwich does not?

1. _____

2. What must all of the following be able to have done to them? stereo, binoculars, high jump bar, sails, air conditioners?

2. _____

3. What is the main duty of stenographers in an office and students at a lecture?

3. _____

4. What power is improved by the microscope, the telescope, and radar?

4. _____

5. What are a detective, a scientist, and a historian all especially trained to do?

5. _____

6. In what special way will a person in semi-darkness look about in order to see better?

6. _____

7. What kind of special room are you likely to find in the buildings of drug companies, electronics firms, universities, and hospitals?

7. _____

8. What is needed for a person to see bacteria, molecules, and the cells of living things?

8. _____

9. How must a person usually work in order to get a job finished thoroughly and well?

9. _____

10. What is less true of history, philosophy, and psychology than of chemistry, biology and physics?

10. _____

GRAMMAR

A. As you know, some words can be used as a noun or as a verb. Most of these words are spelled the same and pronounced the same. Some of these words are spelled the same but are not pronounced the same. Here is one example:

NOUN	VERB
IN sult	in SULT

When the word **insult** is a noun, the accent is on the first syllable. When **insult** is a verb, the accent is on the second syllable.

How do you pronounce **insult** in each of the following sentences? Print the word in the space to show which syllable is accented. (Hint: if the word has **a**, **an**, or **the** before it, it is always a noun.)

1. The queen felt it was an **insult** when the visitor did not bow before her.

1. _____

2. When people **insult** me, I am upset.

2. _____

The lesson word **record** can be either a noun or a verb. The noun is pronounced **REC ord**. The verb is pronounced **re CORD**. How do you pronounce **record** in each of the following sentences? Print the word in the space to show which syllable is accented.

1. The duty of stenographers is to **record** what they hear.

   1. _____

2. The **record** shows that Smith was the best batter in the league.

   2. _____

Here are three other words of the same type.

NOUN	VERB
PROG ress	pro GRESS
PER fect	per FECT
AD dress	ad DRESS

Choose one of these words and write it in one sentence **as a noun** and in a second sentence **as a verb**.

1. (Noun) _____

_____

2. (Verb) _____

_____

B. Form new words by following the directions. Then write the new words in the sentences.

1. Change **adjust** to a noun by adding the suffix **ment**. _____
   When the family moved, Sally had no trouble making an

   _____ to the new neighborhood.

2. Change **diligently** to an adjective by dropping the suffix **ly**. _____
   A _____ person usually has less trouble than a lazy person in finding a job.

3. Change **investigate** to a noun by dropping the final **e** and adding the suffix
   ion. _____
   The police completed their _____ of the case.

4. Change **observation** to a verb by dropping **ation** and adding a final e.

_____

Thousands of people stayed up late to _____ the comet.

5. Change **scientific** to the noun that is the name of a school subject.

_____

Launching a satellite requires knowledge of many branches of

_____ .

WORDLORE

The Dictionary

Below is the entry for the word **instrument**. Read the entry. Then, answer the questions that follow.

> **in stru ment** (in′ strə mənt), _n._ **1** a mechanical device that is portable, of simple construction, and usually operated by hand; tool: _a dentist's instruments._ **2** device for producing musical sounds: _wind instruments, stringed instruments._ **3** device for measuring, recording, or controlling. A compass and sextant are instruments of navigation. **4** thing with or by which something is done; person made use of by another; means: _The alderman proved to be merely an instrument of the mayor._ **5** a formal legal document, such as a contract, deed, or grant. _-v.t._ equip with instruments, especially for recording scientific data: _a fully instrumented missile._ [< Latin _instrumentum_ < _instruere_ prepare, equip, build < _in-_ on + _struere_ to pile, build]

1. How many syllables does **instrument** have? _____

2. You know that **instrument** can be a noun. What other part of speech can **instrument** be? _____

3. What is the special legal meaning that **instrument** can have? _____

_____

4. What two instruments of navigation are named? _____

5. What ancient language does **instrument** come from? _____

6. What are the meanings of the Latin word _instruere?_ _____

Here is a reading passage that contains some of the lesson words. Read the passage. Then answer the questions that follow it.

The astronauts orbited in space. Something went wrong with an **instrument** of navigation. The commander of the crew began to **investigate** the cause of the problem. He issued orders to the crew. The orders were obeyed **diligently.** As a result of his **observation,** the commander felt that the trouble lay with a fuse hidden in a dark corner of the capsule. He **peered** into the dark corner and saw that the fuse was burned out. The fuse was replaced and the crew began to **adjust** the course of the capsule by firing rockets. The main purpose of the mission was to collect **scientific** data about the upper atmosphere. The two members of the crew whose main task was to **record** their findings, began once again to do so.

1. What trouble arose aboard the capsule?

   _____

   _____

2. Who began to investigate the cause of the problem?

   _____

3. How were the orders to the crew obeyed?

   _____

4. Where did the commander finally have to peer to locate the trouble?

   _____

5. What did the crew have to do when the repair had been made?

   _____

   _____

6. What was the main purpose of the mission?

_____

7. How many members of the crew were assigned to record data?

_____

WRITING

There is a lot about science in the news. There are news items about the search for new drugs and other cures and treatments for illness, about the space shuttle and outer space, about computers, about diet and exercise, about the environment, and many other scientific topics.

In a short paragraph, write a purely imaginary news report about a discovery or event in some field of science. Try to use at least three of the lesson words or forms of them in your paragraph.

_____

_____

_____

_____

_____

_____

_____

See how many of the lesson words or forms of them you can find in newspapers, magazines, books, and other printed matter. If you find a word in newspapers or magazines that are ready to be thrown away, clip out the article or paragraph in which the word occurs. If you find any of the words in a book, copy the sentence in which the word appears. Then make a note of the title and author of the book. Your teacher will tell you when to bring your collection to class.

LESSON 6

LOOK AT THE PICTURE

What Did You See?

1. What part of the world is this person probably from?

_____

2. How is she dressed?

_____

3. What do you notice about her hair?

_____

4. Use a word or phrase to describe the expression on her face.

_____

5. What does she appear to be doing?

_____

_____

6. Use a word or phrase to describe the room.

_____

PRONUNCIATION

Here are ten lesson words suggested by the picture. With the help of your teacher, pronounce each word.

ancient   (ān′ shənt)
attire   (ə tīr′)
ceremony   (ser′ ə mō′ nē)
fragile   (fraj′ əl)
illumination   (i lü′ mə nā′ shən)
oriental   (ôr′ ē en′ tl)
ornament   (ôr′ nə mənt)
solemn   (sol′ əm)
solitary   (sol′ ə ter′ ē)
tradition   (trə dish′ ən)

SPELLING

Be sure you know how to spell each word. Here are the words given in sentences. Letters are missing from each word. First put the missing letters where they belong. Then write each complete word in the space.

1. In some cities of Europe there are modern buildings sharply contrasting with AN__ __ __NT ones standing alongside.

1. _____

2. The knights went into battle in dress of armor, an A__ __IRE that made movement clumsy and difficult.

2. _____

3. The marriage C__ __ __MONY differs in various ways in different places of the world. Everywhere, though, it is a serious and important custom.

3. _____

4. The thin glass vase was very FRA__ __LE. Therefore, it had to be wrapped carefully so that it would not break.

4. _____

5. The I__ __ __M__NATION given by electric bulbs is much better than the light given by candles.

5. _____

6. The OR__ __ __TAL world of Japan, Korea and China is still different in many ways from the western world.

6. _____

7. In general, she dressed very plainly, without jewelry or other decoration. She did, however, wear one small silver O__ __ __MENT at her throat.

7. _____

8. The movie was a sad and SOLE__ __one. There was not a sound of laughter in the audience from beginning to end.

8. _____

9. There was not a person to be seen in the streets except for a SOL__T__RY figure, an old man struggling with great difficulty through the deep snow.

9. _____

10. It is a TR__D__ __ION among a number of different peoples to have occasional days of fasting. This age-old practice is thought by some to be good for the health.

10. _____

How Do These Words Go With the Picture?

How well can you see the connection between each word and the picture? For as many words as you can, explain briefly how the word goes with the picture.

1. **ancient** _____

2. **attire** _____

3. **ceremony** _____

4. **fragile** _____

5. **illumination** _____

6. **oriental** _____

7. **ornament** _____

8. **solemn** _____

9. solitary _____

10. tradition _____

CONTEXT CLUES

Here are ten passages. The lesson word that completes each passage has been left out. See if you can write the proper word in each blank. Look for helpful clues in the passage. If you are not absolutely sure, take a good guess.

1. Some people prefer fluorescent tubes for _____ while others like the light of bulbs better.

2. Everywhere there are astonishing structures built by the people of long ago. These monuments tell us that even in _____ times people had advanced building skills.

3. The lighthouse keeper lived alone in his tower most of the year. Yet, he seemed to enjoy this _____ life, not missing the company of other people.

4. The countries of the West have long led those of the East in industry. Recently, though, _____ nations have taken the lead in the production of automobiles, cameras, stereos, and many other products.

5. Metal is strong and does not break easily, but glass is _____ and can shatter into a thousand pieces when dropped.

6. It is the custom to eat turkey on Thanksgiving. This _____ goes back to Colonial times.

7. Everyone became _____ when news of the approaching hurricane was heard on the radio. Then, it was announced that the storm had turned out to sea, and a smile broke out on every face.

8. The dress of the Eskimos is designed for protection against extreme cold. Their _____ includes a fur jacket and hood and sealskin boots.

9. Graduation is an important formal occasion. It is usually marked by a

    _____ that includes the wearing of caps and gowns, appropriate music, speeches, awards, and the presentation of diplomas.

10. They began to put the decorations on the Christmas tree. Finally, the last

    _____ was put in place.

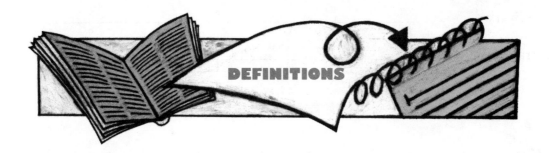

DEFINITIONS

Most words have several meanings. Some words can be used as two or more parts of speech. The Table shows one part of speech and one meaning for each word. Study this information. After doing so, review your answers to Context Clues. Correct any errors.

Word	Part of Speech	Definition
ancient	adjective	belonging to times long past; very old
attire	noun	clothing; the way a person is dressed
ceremony	noun	a special set of acts for special occasions, such as weddings, graduations, and inaugurations
fragile	adjective	easily broken or damaged; frail; delicate
illumination	noun	the amount of light; lighting up
oriental	adjective	Eastern; relating to the countries of Asia as opposed to those of Europe and America
ornament	noun	a decoration; a pretty object
solemn	adjective	serious; sad
solitary	adjective	alone; single; lonely
tradition	noun	the beliefs or customs handed down from the past

THINKING

Headlines

Here are five imaginary newspaper headlines. In the space following each, write the lesson word most likely to appear in the news story that follows each headline.

1. Exhibition of art of Japan and China to open   1. _____
2. All electrical power fails over wide area   2. _____
3. New clothing styles now being shown in stores   3. _____
4. Millions watch inauguration of President   4. _____
5. Archaeologists unearth ruins dating 500 B.C.   5. _____

Matching

Alongside each word in Column I, write the letter for the word or phrase from Column II that best goes with it.

I   II

A

_____ 1. ancient   a. glassware
_____ 2. tradition   b. funeral
_____ 3. fragile   c. wonton soup
_____ 4. solemn   d. prehistoric fossils
_____ 5. oriental   e. July 4 celebration

B

_____ 1. attire   a. hermit
_____ 2. ceremony   b. searchlight
_____ 3. solitary   c. band uniform
_____ 4. ornament   d. launching of a big new ship
_____ 5. illumination   e. earring

GRAMMAR

A. The words **attire** and **ornament** can be either a noun or a verb. Tell whether the word in heavy type in each of the following sentences is a noun or a verb.

1. Since it was bitterly cold outside, she **attired** herself in her warmest clothing.   1. _____

2. The room was decorated with glittering **ornaments** from all over the world.   2. _____

3. The shop owner **ornaments** his store windows with flowers in the spring, pumpkins in the fall, and artificial snow in the winter.   3. _____

4. The chief's head was **ornamented** with a bonnet of colorful feathers.   4. _____

5. The **attire** worn by people often tells us what they are, as in the cases of police officers, clergymen, construction workers, and forest rangers.   5. _____

6. Some people prefer informal, comfortable **attire.**   6. _____

7. She always **attires** herself in something green, her favorite color.   7. _____

8. In India, many women **attire** themselves in flowing robes.   8. _____

9. In preparation for the interview, she had **attired** herself in
her best outfit and was ready to leave.   9. _____

10. The little children have **ornamented** themselves with grown-
up jewelry and clothing.   10. _____

B. Form new words by following the directions. Then write the new words
in the sentences.

1. Change **ceremony** to an adjective by changing the y to an i and adding the

   suffix **al.** _____

   The _____ procession moved through the center of
   town.

2. Change **ceremony** to a plural by changing the y to an i and adding **es.**

   _____

   In most countries, there are birth, marriage, and death _____ .

3. Change **solemn** to an adverb by adding the suffix **ly.** _____

   People listened _____ while the sermon was being
   delivered.

4. Change **ornament** to an adjective by adding the suffix **al.** _____

   In Spain and Japan, women used to wear _____
   combs in their hair.

5. Change **illumination** to a verb. _____

   Powerful searchlights were used to _____ the field.

C. Form the plural of each of the following nouns in the same way you
formed the plural of **ceremony.**

Singular	Plural
tragedy	_____
lady	_____
sky	_____
army	_____
body	_____

Change the following adjectives to adverbs in the same way you changed **solemn** to an adverb.

Adjective	Adverb
false	_____
meek	_____
harsh	_____
kind	_____
soft	_____

Use any two of the new words you have formed in sentences of your own.

1. _____

2. _____

WORDLORE

Synonyms and Antonyms

Each lesson word below is followed by three words. One of these words is either a synonym or an antonym. Write the synonym or antonym in the space provided. Tell which it is by using S for synonym and A for antonym.

1. ORNAMENT: decoration, flood, library   _____ _____
2. FRAGILE: expensive, old, unbreakable   _____ _____
3. SOLITARY: alone, precious, sweet   _____ _____
4. ANCIENT: tall, modern, fallen   _____ _____
5. ATTIRE: care, shabbiness, dress   _____ _____

The Dictionary

Below is the dictionary entry for the word **ceremony.** Look it over; then answer the questions.

cer e mo ny (ser′ ə mō′nē), *n., pl.* **-nies. 1** a special act or set of acts to be done on special occasions such as weddings, funerals, graduations, or holidays: *a marriage ceremony.* See synonym study below. **2** very polite conduct; way of conducting oneself that follows all the rules of polite social behavior. *The old gentleman showed us to the door with a great deal of ceremony.* **3** attention to forms and customs; formality: *the traditional ceremony of the royal court.* **4 stand on ceremony,** be too polite; be very formal. **5** an empty form; meaningless formality. [< Latin *caerimonia* rite] **Syn. 1 Ceremony, rite** mean a set of dignified and usually traditional practices followed on special occasions. **Ceremony** applies to the observances or procedure used on religious, public, or other solemn occasions: *The graduation ceremony was inspiring.* **Rite** applies to a fixed ceremony, in which both the actions and the words are prescribed: *A priest administered the last rites to the dying victims of the fire.*

1. What letter is used to show how the **c** in **ceremony** is pronounced? _____

2. Notice the four letters shown for the plural. Write the whole word for the plural form. _____

3. What four special occasions are mentioned as examples? _____
   _____

4. What sentence is given to show how **ceremony** can name a certain type of behavior? _____
   _____
   _____

5. What ancient language does **ceremony** come from? _____

6. What is a near synonym for **ceremony**? _____

READING COMPREHENSION

Here is a reading passage that contains some of the lesson words. Read the passage. Then answer the questions that follow it.

Spaghetti is commonly thought of as a food belonging to the **tradition** of Italy. However, spaghetti was probably first created in China in **ancient** times. It is believed that Marco Polo introduced spaghetti to Italy from China.

Marco Polo was a great traveler who was born in Venice about 1254. As a young man, he journeyed to China with his father and uncle. They were received by the famous ruler, Kublai Khan, with warm welcome and great **ceremony**. Later, Marco Polo was appointed to high office in the court, the **solitary** outsider to have such power.

Until the times of Polo, European knowledge of **oriental** lands was almost nonexistent. Polo brought back information about the beliefs, customs, and **attire** of the Chinese people of the time. He also brought back **fragile** samples of their arts and crafts. It is also believed that he was given samples of lovely, precious **ornaments**.

With the close friendship between Marco Polo and Kublai Khan, it must have been a sad and **solemn** occasion for both men when Polo took his leave to return to his homeland.

1. Where is spaghetti thought of as a traditional food?

   _____

2. Where was spaghetti probably created in ancient times?

   _____

3. What role did Marco Polo play in the history of spaghetti?

   _____

   _____

4. How was Marco Polo received by Kublai Khan?

   _____

5. What solitary role did Marco Polo play in the court of Kublai Khan?

   _____

6. How much did Europeans know of oriental lands before the time of Marco Polo?

   _____

7. What were some of the kinds of information and gifts Marco Polo brought

   back with him? _____

   _____

   _____

8. How did Marco Polo and Kublai Khan probably feel when they parted?

   _____

WRITING

   Write a short paragraph about some ceremony or tradition that you know about from your own experience or from your reading. Try to use at least three of the lesson words or forms of them in your paragraph.

   _____
   _____
   _____

See how many of the lesson words or forms of them you can find in newspapers, magazines, books, and other printed matter. If you find a word in newspapers or magazines that are ready to be thrown away, clip out the article or paragraph in which the word occurs. If you find any of the words in a book, copy the sentence in which the word appears. Then make a note of the title and author of the book. Your teacher will tell you when to bring your collection to class.

LESSON 7

LOOK AT THE PICTURE

What Did You See?

1. Where is this person?

2. What special equipment is he wearing?

_____

3. What is he doing?

_____

_____

4. Why is he wearing heavy rubber gloves?

_____

5. What is the white "cloud" just above his head?

_____

6. What do you see growing?

_____

7. What is your guess as to why the person is doing what he is doing?

_____

_____

PRONUNCIATION

Here are ten lesson words suggested by the picture. With the help of your teacher, pronounce each word.

apparatus (ap′ ə rat′ əs)
aquatic (ə kwot′ ik)
descend (di send′)
edible (ed′ ə bəl)
exhale (eks hāl′)
intrepid (in trep′ id)
marine (mə rēn′)
murky (mėr′ kē)
vegetation (vej′ ə tā′ shən)
visibility (viz′ ə bil′ ə tē)

SPELLING

Be sure you know how to spell each word. Here are the words given in sentences. Letters are missing from each word. First put the missing letters where they belong. Then write each complete word in the space.

1. The fire fighters arrived on the scene with all their A__ __ __ __ATUS.

   1. _____

2. Oceans, lakes, and ponds are the scene of such sports as swimming, water skiing, sailing, snorkeling, and fishing. These A__ __ __TIC sports provide fun for millions of people.

   2. _____

3. The plane was approaching the airport and it was time for the pilot to bring the plane down. The jet liner began to DE__ __END gently through the clouds.

   3. _____

4. By watching birds and animals, primitive people learned which things were all right for them to eat. They learned which berries, fruits, and nuts were ED__B__E and which they should not try to eat.

   4. _____

5. We breathe in oxygen. We EX__ __ __E carbon dioxide.

   5. _____

6. You can't be a fearful person to be an astronaut, a police officer, or an underwater explorer. Only INTR__ __ __D people can face such dangers and uncertainties.

   6. _____

7. The sea is rich in plant and animal life and in minerals. That is one reason for the M__R__NE studies that go on all the time.

   7. _____

8. It was a dark, misty night. Drivers had trouble seeing through the M__R__Y air.

   8. _____

9. Plants adapt themselves to all kinds of conditions. There is some VE__ __ __ATION even in deserts and the Arctic wastelands.

   9. _____

10. Because of the heavy fog, we could not see three feet ahead of us. We decided to pull over to the side of the road until VI__ __B__L__TY improved.

    10. _____

How Do These Words Go With the Picture?

How well can you see the connection between each word and the picture? For as many words as you can, explain briefly how the word goes with the picture.

1. apparatus _____

2. aquatic _____

3. descend _____

4. edible _____

5. exhale _____

6. intrepid _____

7. marine _____

8. murky _____

9. vegetation _____

10. visibility _____

CONTEXT CLUES

Here are ten passages. The lesson word that completes each passage has been left out. See if you can write the proper word in each blank. Look for helpful clues in the passage. If you are not absolutely sure, take a good guess.

1. Grasses and other _____ grew plentifully in the meadows. Sheep and cattle grazed on these plants.

2. Swimming and diving are important Olympic sports. The Americans often win many medals in these _____ events.

3. Everybody looked forward to eating the delicious foods at the picnic. How disappointed they were to find that everything was covered with ants and other bugs and therefore not _____!

4. The air was clean and _____ was excellent. The mountain climbers could see for miles around.

5. The parachute opened and the jumper began to _____ gently towards the earth.

6. The road crew arrived on the scene with all their equipment. Their
   _____ included jackhammers, cement mixers, and a
   steamroller.

7. Miners are equipped with powerful lights. With the aid of these, they can
   see better through the _____ dust and darkness of the
   mine shafts.

8. The swimmer was instructed to breathe in through her mouth and to
   _____ through her nose.

9. Some people are driven to acts of bravery. These _____
   adventurers climb Mount Everest, explore the Antarctic, and rocket into
   outer space.

10. Most mammals live on land but some live in the sea. Among these
    _____ animals are whales, dolphins, and porpoises.

DEFINITIONS

Most words have several meanings. Some words can be used as two or more
parts of speech. The Table shows one part of speech and one meaning for each
word. Study this information. Review your answers to Context Clues. Correct
any errors.

Word	Part of Speech	Definition
apparatus	noun	the tools, machinery, or other equipment for a particular use
aquatic	adjective	having to do with water
descend	verb	to go or come down
edible	adjective	fit to eat
exhale	verb	to breathe out
intrepid	adjective	very brave; fearless
marine	adjective	having to do with the sea; of the sea
murky	adjective	dark; gloomy; hazy
vegetation	noun	plant life; growing plants
visibility	noun	the degree to which things can be seen

THINKING

Odd Word Out

In this exercise, one of the list words is shown in capital letters. It is followed by four other words. Three of these words belong with the capitalized word. One does not. Cross out the "stranger."

1. AQUATIC: fishing, walking, sailing, snorkeling
2. DESCEND: hail, rain, snow, wind
3. INTREPID: Columbus, David, Lindbergh, Shakespeare
4. MURKY: sunlight, cave, fog, twilight
5. VEGETATION: cactus, grass, water, weeds

Matching

Alongside each word in Column I, write the word or phrase from Column II that best goes with it.

	I	II
_____	1. apparatus	lungs
_____	2. edible	coral reef
_____	3. exhale	fire engine
_____	4. marine	torch
_____	5. visibility	tomato

Word Quiz

1. Give two lesson words that have something to do with eating.

   _____   _____

2. Give two lesson words that have something to do with seeing.

   _____   _____

3. Give two lesson words that have something to do with water.

   _____   _____

4. Give one lesson word that has something to do with breathing.

   _____

5. Give two lesson words that would have something to do with a person who has climbed to the top of Mount Everest.

   _____   _____

GRAMMAR

A. Practice using forms of the verb **descend**. Use the proper form in each sentence.

1. Monkeys ascend and _____ among the trees by swinging from branch to branch.

2. Every morning the maintenance person _____ to the basement to check the boiler.

3. You can _____ to the main floor by using the escalators or the elevator.

4. The plane was _____ to the runway when it was hit by a gust of wind.

5. The divers _____ to the ocean floor and searched for the wreckage.

B. Form new words by following the directions. Then write the new words in the sentences.

1. Change the verb **descend** to a noun by changing the final **d** to a **t**. _____

   The parachute floated down in a slow _____.

2. Change the noun **visibility** to an adjective by dropping the suffix **ility** and adding **le**. _____

   In the heavy fog, the shore was not _____.

3. Add the prefix **in** to the word you formed in 2 to form a word meaning "not able to be seen." _____

   In the heavy fog, the shore was _____.

4. Change **edible** to a word meaning "not fit for eating" by adding the prefix **in**.

   _____

   The meat was undercooked and _____.

5. Change the noun **vegetation** to a verb by dropping the suffix **ion** and adding a final **e**. _____

   Some plants _____ by spreading underground runners, while others drop seeds.

WORDLORE

Synonyms and Antonyms

Each lesson word below is followed by three words. One of these three words is either a synonym or an antonym. Write the synonym or antonym in the space provided. Tell which it is by using S for synonym and A for antonym.

1. APPARATUS: exercise, equipment, error   _____ _____
2. EXHALE: inhale, digest, suffocate   _____ _____
3. MURKY: sad, old, dim   _____ _____
4. INTREPID: daring, foolish, handsome   _____ _____
5. DESCEND: arrive, ascend, approve   _____ _____

The Dictionary

Below is the dictionary entry for the word **murky**. Look it over. Then answer the questions.

> murk y (mèr′ kē), *adj.*, murk i er, murk i est. **1** dark; gloomy: *a murky prison.* **2** very thick and dark; misty; hazy: *murky smoke.* **3** hard to understand; obscure: *a murky argument. Also,* **mirky.**—murk′ i ly, *adv.*—murk′ i ness, *n.*

1. What word means "more murky"? _____

2. What word means "most murky"? _____

3. Name three of the synonyms given for **murky**.

   _____   _____   _____

4. Write the three examples that are given of **murky** used with a noun.

   _____

   _____

   _____

5. What is the noun form of **murky**? _____

READING COMPREHENSION

Here is a reading passage that contains some of the lesson words. Read the passage. Then answer the questions that follow it.

Jacques Cousteau is a famous **marine** scientist. That branch of science requires the scientist to be an **intrepid** adventurer as well as a searcher after knowledge.

On a ship equipped with all sorts of special **apparatus,** Cousteau and his assistants have studied the seas from the surface to the depths below. With his diving equipment he has been able to **descend** to great depths. There the water is **murky.** Powerful lights help to improve **visibility,** the better to observe fish and **vegetation.**

Of all the gear used by marine scientists such as Cousteau, scuba gear may be the most important. It is interesting to know that the word **scuba** is formed from the first letters of the words "self-contained underwater breathing apparatus." That phrase really tells all about the usefulness of scuba equipment to Jacques Cousteau, marine scientist.

1. In which branch of science does Jacques Cousteau specialize?

_____

2. What character trait does that branch of science require?

_____

3. With what was Cousteau's ship equipped?

_____

4. What kind of study has this ship made possible?

_____

5. Why are powerful lights necessary?

_____

_____

6. How was the word **scuba** formed?

_____

_____

_____

Go to a good dictionary and look up the word **acronym**. Write a short paragraph in which you define this interesting word and in which you give at least two examples of acronyms.

_____

_____

_____

_____

_____

_____

See how many of the lesson words or forms of them you can find in newspapers, magazines, books, and other printed matter. If you find a word in newspapers or magazines that are ready to be thrown away, clip out the article or paragraph in which the word occurs. If you find any of the words in a book, copy the sentence in which the word appears. Then make a note of the title and author of the book. Your teacher will tell you when to bring your collection to class.

LESSON 8

LOOK AT THE PICTURE

What Did You See?

1. Is this scene in the country or in a park in a large city? How do you know?

_____

_____

2. What is the probable time of year?

_____

3. How many families do there seem to be? How do the members of the families match up nicely?

_____

_____

4. What do you think the people in the back are carrying? What does this tell you?

_____

_____

5. What is the older girl in the front carrying? What does this tell you?

_____

_____

6. How do the two families seem to be getting along?

_____

_____

7. What is the mood of all the people in this scene? Why?

_____

_____

PRONUNCIATION

Here are ten lesson words suggested by the picture. With the help of your teacher, pronounce each word.

anticipate   (an tis′ ə pāt)
balmy   (bä′ mē)
companionship   (kəm pan′ yən ship)
escape   (e skāp′)
excursion   (ek skėr′ zhən)
harmony   (här′ mə nē)
leisure   (lē′ zhər)
picnic   (pik′ nik)
recreation   (rek′ rē ā′ shən)
stroll   (strōl)

SPELLING

Be sure you know how to spell each word. Here are the words given in sentences. Letters are missing from each word. First put the missing letters where they belong. Then write each complete word in the space.

1. It was June and the children began to ANTI___ ___ ___ ___TE the summer vacation. They wanted to swim and play ball.

   1._____

2. In May come B___ ___MY days, with a warming sun and gentle breezes.

   2._____

3. The old woman lived alone without human friends. The only COMPA___ ___ ___ ___SHIP she knew was that given by her dog and cat.

   3._____

4. At least once a year most people want to get away from their regular activities and surroundings. They want to E___ ___APE and have a change of scenery.

   4._____

5. The club discussed what kind of short trip they would take this year. They decided on an EX___ ___ ___SION to the State Park.

   5._____

6. At first there was a lot of disagreement and argument. Finally, differences were ironed out and a decision was arrived at in peace and HAR___ ___N___ .

   6._____

7. All week long he worked very hard. He looked forward to the weekend which he could spend in rest and L___ ___ ___URE.

   7._____

8. First, the tablecloth was spread on the grass. The utensils were laid out and the food was taken out of the basket. Everybody sat down to enjoy the P___ ___NIC.

   8._____

9. "All work and no play makes Jack a dull boy." Therefore, almost everybody likes to set aside time for R___ ___ ___ ___ATION. Some like active games, while others prefer reading or listening to music.

   9._____

10. Maria and Dolores decided to take a STR___ ___ ___ in the park, enjoying the spring day.

    10._____

How Do These Words Go With the Picture?

How well can you see the connection between each word and the picture? For as many words as you can, explain briefly how the word goes with the picture.

1. anticipate   _____

2. balmy   _____

3. companionship   _____

4. escape   _____

5. excursion   _____

6. harmony   _____

7. leisure   _____

8. picnic   _____

9. recreation   _____

10. stroll   _____

CONTEXT CLUES

Here are ten passages. The lesson word that completes each passage has been left out. See if you can write the proper word in each blank. Look for helpful clues in the passage. If you are not absolutely sure, take a good guess.

1. We decided to take along a _____ lunch to have on the roadside. That way we could enjoy the outdoors while eating instead of going into a restaurant.

2. The weather forecasters did not _____ the tornado. Not expecting the storm, nobody prepared for it.

3. To get away from the problems and worries of life, some people bury themselves in adventure stories. Others like to _____ by watching television.

4. On a Sunday, crowds like to _____ along the boardwalk. As they walk, they enjoy the ocean view and the fresh sea air.

5. People usually enjoy friendship with others. However, once in a while everybody prefers to be alone, without human _____.

6. In the life of every family there are some periods of squabbling and disagreement. More frequently, families get along in _____ and peace.

7. In the summer, swimming and tennis are popular forms of play. In the winter, skiing and ice-skating provide _____ for many.

8. In the morning, the weather was unpleasant, with cold winds and rain. In the afternoon, it turned mild and _____, with clear skies and a golden sun.

9. Last year, the class went to Washington D.C., for its annual trip. This year, we have chosen a boat ride up the Hudson River for our

_____ .

10. All week long, Richard went to school and did his homework. Weekends and holidays he worked in the drugstore. He had no _____ time at all.

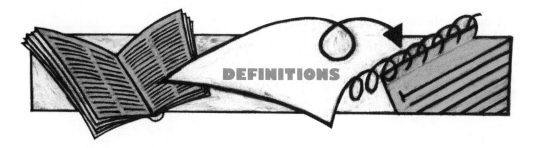

DEFINITIONS

Most words have several meanings. Some words can be used as two or more parts of speech. The Table shows one part of speech and one meaning for each word. Study this information. After doing so, review your answers to Context Clues. Correct any errors.

Word	Part of Speech	Definition
anticipate	verb	to expect; look forward to
balmy	adjective	mild; gentle; soothing; pleasant
companionship	noun	fellowship; comradeship; company
escape	verb	to get away from; get free from
excursion	noun	a short journey or trip, often taken by a number of people together
harmony	noun	getting on well together; agreement; pleasant and peaceful relationship
leisure	noun	the time free from required work in which persons can do as they wish for enjoyment or just rest
picnic	noun	a meal in the open air, with food brought along
recreation	noun	play; amusement; games
stroll	verb	to take a quiet walk for pleasure

THINKING

Word Quiz

Show how well you can use the words as part of your thinking. Answer each question by writing one of the lesson words.

1. People are worried about ants, bees, and rain.
    What kind of meal are they going to have?   1._____

2. If scouts are going on a hike, what kind of walking are they NOT likely to do?   2._____

3. People in the streets are wearing heavy coats
    and warm hats, boots or galoshes, and gloves.
    What word can NOT be used to describe the
    weather?   3._____

4. What do people often seek in having a pet dog?   4._____

5. A boy spends as much time as he can watching
    sci-fi television programs and movies like *Star
    Trek* and *Star Wars*. What is he probably trying
    to do?   5._____

Sentence Sense

In each of the following sentences, one word does not make good sense. Cross it out and write a lesson word that will make the sentence sensible. Use the spaces to the right. (Note: more than one lesson word may make sense in some sentences.)

1. Weekends are usually a time of work. Most peo-
    ple do whatever they feel like without thinking
    about the clock.   1._____

2. The two nations signed a peace treaty and made
    many friendly agreements of benefit to both.
    Then followed a period of calm warfare be-
    tween them.   2._____

3. Our club went on a trip to the museum. We
    learned a lot and had a good time, too. All in
    all, it was a fine illness.   3._____

4. If you forget rain, you will wear a raincoat and
    carry an umbrella.   4._____

5. My favorite kinds of labor are fishing, movies,
    and just talking with good friends.   5._____

GRAMMAR

A. The words **escape**, **picnic**, and **stroll** can be used as either nouns or verbs in sentences. Tell whether the word in heavy type in the following sentences is a noun or a verb.

1. People **escape** from the cares of the day by playing board games in the evening.   1. _____

2. **Escape** can also be found through active sports.   2. _____

3. Everybody enjoyed the **picnic.**   3. _____

4. Many families **picnicked** in the park.   4. _____

5. Vacationers were **picnicking** by the roadside.   5. _____

6. Do you enjoy **picnics?**   6. _____

7. Window-shoppers **strolled** along the avenue.   7. _____

8. A quiet **stroll** in the country is a good way to relax.   8. _____

9. The boy **strolls** along the side of the brook looking for frogs.   9. _____

10. He always looked forward to the **strolls** he took every Sunday afternoon.   10. _____

A SPELLING NOTE: Did you notice the spelling of **picnicked** and **picnicking?** When **picnic** is used as a verb and **ed** or **ing** is added, a **k** comes after the final **c.** The same rule applies to **panic** and **mimic.**

panic	mimic
panicked	mimicked
panicking	mimicking

B. The suffix **ship** means "a general condition." It is added to some words to form a new word, as in **companion + ship = companionship.** Add the suffix **ship** to each of the following words to form a new word.

friend   _____

scholar   _____

partner   _____

relation   _____

hard   _____

C. Form new words by following the directions. Then write the new words in the sentences.

1. Change **leisure** to an adverb by adding **ly.** _____

   The picnickers strolled through the park in a _____ manner.

2. Change **anticipate** to a noun by dropping the final **e** and adding **ion**.

_____

We all looked forward to the party with great

_____.

3. Change **harmony** to an adjective by changing the y to an **i** and adding **ous**.

_____

The United States has a _____ relationship with Canada.

4. Change the adjective you formed from **harmony** to an adverb by adding **ly**.

_____

The quartet sang _____.

WORDLORE

Synonyms

Each lesson word is followed by three other words. Two of these words are synonyms of the lesson word. Write the two synonyms in the spaces provided. Then choose one of the synonyms and write it in a sentence of your own.

1. BALMY: soothing, distant, gentle

Synonyms   1. _____   2. _____

Sentence   _____

_____

2. HARMONY: darkness, agreement, peacefulness

Synonyms   1. _____   2. _____

Sentence   _____

_____

3. ANTICIPATE: expect, retreat, await

Synonyms   1. _____   2. _____

Sentence   _____

_____

4. EXCURSION: trip, outing, settlement

Synonyms   1. _____   2. _____

Sentence   _____

_____

5. COMPANIONSHIP: happiness, friendship, comradeship

Synonyms   1. _____   2. _____

Sentence   _____

Rhymes

Have some fun with rhymes. Select a lesson word to complete each of the following rhymes.

1. A Roman, a Greek, a Turk, and a Persian,

   Took off down the Nile on a peaceful _____.

2. The color of foliage inspires the soul

   When during the autumn you go for a _____.

3. I guess I should know what has made me so sick.

   I ate fourteen franks on the Sunday _____.

4. When planning on taking a lengthy trip,

   Don't do it alone. Have _____.

5. When the weather is cold and the wind is not calm, he

   Departs for the South where the weather is _____.

READING COMPREHENSION

Here is a reading passage that contains some of the lesson words. Read the passage. Then answer the questions that follow it.

Sunday was always a day of **leisure** for the Brown family. As spring approached, Mr. and Mrs. Brown decided to take the children on an **excursion** to the zoo on the first Sunday in April. The forecast was for **balmy** weather. They did not **anticipate** that the forecast might not be right. When Sunday came it turned out to be cloudy and windy.

Nevertheless, all members of the family were in **harmony** in deciding to go ahead with their outing. They did make one change. Instead of taking a **picnic** lunch to eat in the park, they would have lunch at the zoo cafeteria.

At the zoo, the monkey house was, as always, the first stop. They enjoyed the way the chimpanzees seemed to enjoy the **companionship** both of each other and of the human spectators, for all of whom they put on a show of antics, tricks, and funny faces. Soon, however, the monkey house became too crowded with people and the Browns decided to **escape** to the fresh air.

They went outdoors and visited the seals which were constantly in and out of the water. Then they decided to **stroll** over to the polar bear area. The bears were also busy in the water.

Then, the whole family was hungry and they had lunch. After lunch, the children wanted to finish up the day with some **recreation** in the playground. They tried the swings, the slides, the seesaws, and the climbing bars. When they had had enough, it was time to go home.

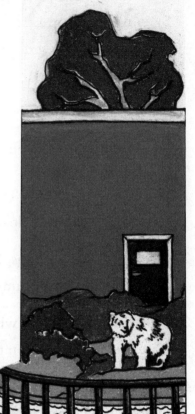

1. Which was always the day of leisure for the Brown family?

   _____

2. When was the family going on an excursion to the zoo?

   _____

3. What kind of weather did they anticipate?

   _____

4. What kind of weather did they get?

   _____

5. How much disagreement was there about whether they should go to the zoo in view of the weather?

   _____

6. What one change in plans was made?

   _____

   _____

7. Whose companionship did the chimpanzees seem to enjoy?

_____

_____

8. How did they show their enjoyment?

_____

_____

9. How did the children want to wind up the day?

_____

_____

WRITING

Write a short paragraph about you and your best friend. Try to use at least three of the lesson words or forms of them in your paragraph.

_____

_____

_____

_____

_____

_____

_____

_____

ASSIGNMENT

See how many of the lesson words or forms of them you can find in newspapers, magazines, books, and other printed matter. If you find a word in newspapers or magazines that are ready to be thrown away, clip out the article or paragraph in which the word occurs. If you find any of the words in a book, copy the sentence in which the word appears. Then make a note of the title and author of the book. Your teacher will tell you when to bring your collection to class.

REVIEW LESSONS 5-8

LOOK AT THE PICTURE

What Did You See?

1. Where are these people?

   _____

2. Why are they there?

   _____

3. What do they see?

   _____

4. What do you especially notice about the group?

   _____

Here are the forty words you have learned so much about in Lessons 5-8. First, review the list by saying each word aloud. Then go on to the review exercises and refer to this list as you need to.

adjust	ancient	apparatus	anticipate
diligently	attire	aquatic	balmy
instrument	ceremony	descend	companionship
investigate	fragile	edible	escape
laboratory	illumination	exhale	excursion
microscope	oriental	intrepid	harmony
observation	ornament	marine	leisure
peer	solemn	murky	picnic
record	solitary	vegetation	recreation
scientific	tradition	visibility	stroll

How Do These Words Go With the Picture?

Here are three lesson words. Briefly explain the connection of each to the picture.

1. **ancient** _____

2. **observation** _____

3. **intrepid** _____

Now select from the review list five other lesson words that you feel are connected to the picture. Write each word and briefly explain the connection.

_____ _____

_____ _____

_____ _____

_____ _____

_____ _____

Ideas

You are given words suggesting a general idea. For each, select three lesson words that are closely connected with the idea. Write the words. Then choose one word and write it in a sentence of your own.

1. LEARNING

   Words: _____ _____ _____

   Sentence: _____

   _____

2. FEELINGS

Words: _____ _____ _____

Sentence: _____

_____

3. ENVIRONMENT

Words: _____ _____ _____

Sentence: _____

_____

4. HEALTH

Words: _____ _____ _____

Sentence: _____

_____

Scrambled Words and Anagrams

Here are five lesson words with the letters scrambled. On line **a**, write the letters in the correct order. On line **b**, follow the instructions for each word.

1. REPE   a._____

   Add *C* to the letters of your word and use those letters to form a new word meaning "crawl."   b._____

2. TARTIE   a._____

   Add *S* to the letters of your word and use those letters to form a new word meaning "more enjoyable to
   eat."   b._____

3. CAPEES   a._____

   Add *H* to the letters of your word and use those letters to form a new word naming fruit with a fuzzy
   skin.   b._____

4. LTOSRL   a._____

   Add *P* and *E* to the letters of your word and use
   those letters to form a new word meaning "a person
   who takes opinion surveys."   b._____

5. DORECR   a._____

   Add *N* and *E* to the letters of your word and use
   those letters to form a new word meaning "trapped."   b._____

GRAMMAR

A. Write the plurals of these nouns.

1. instrument   _____

2. laboratory (*Be careful!*)   _____

3. ornament   _____

4. excursion   _____

5. stroll   _____

Use any one of the words you have written in a sentence of your own.

_____

_____

B. Change each word to an adjective that will fit sensibly when you write it in the blank space in each sentence.

1. **diligently**

   She was a _____ student who always completed as-signments on time.

2. **ornament**

   Furniture has a practical purpose, but it also is _____, adding the decoration of color and arrangement to a room.

3. **tradition**

   Fireworks displays and parades are the _____ ways of celebrating the Fourth of July.

4. **visibility**

   The power beam of the lighthouse was _____ miles out to sea.

5. **harmony**

   The United States and Canada live next to each other as _____ neighbors.

C. Write the past tense of these verbs.

1. adjust   _____

2. peer   _____

3. record   _____

4. picnic (*Be careful!*)   _____

5. escape   _____

D. Change each word to an adverb that will fit sensibly when you write it in the blank space in each sentence.

1. **solemn**

   Do you _____ swear to tell the truth, the whole truth, and nothing but the truth?

2. **traditional**

   The Fourth of July is _____ celebrated with fireworks displays and parades.

Use any one of the words you have written in a sentence of your own.

_____

_____

The Dictionary

Here is the dictionary entry for **adjust**. Look it over. Answer the questions.

ad just (ə just′), *v.t.* **1** change (something) to make fit; adapt. See synonym study below. **2** put in proper order, position, or relation; arrange: *Please adjust the TV so that the picture doesn't jump.* **3** arrange (differences, discrepancies, etc.) satisfactorily; set right; settle. **4** decide the amount to be paid in settling (a bill, insurance claim, etc.). —*v.i.* **1** adapt oneself; get used *(to): Some wild animals never adjust to captivity.* **2** have its angle, focus, height, etc., changed so as to fit different users: *The new camera has a lens that adjusts automatically.* [< Old French *ajuster* < *a-* for + *just* straight] —**ad just′ a ble,** *adj.* —**ad just′ a bly,** *adv.* —**ad just′ er, ad jus′ tor,** *n.*
Syn. *v.t.* **1** Adjust, adapt, accommodate have in common the idea of fitting one thing or person to another. **Adjust** emphasizes the idea of matching one thing to another: *The teacher adjusted the seat to the height of the child.* **Adapt** emphasizes the idea of making minor changes in a thing (or person) to make it fit, suit, or fit into something: *I adapted the pattern to the material.* **Accommodate** emphasizes that the things to be fitted together are so different that one must be subordinated to the other: *I have to accommodate my desires to my income.*

1. How many syllables does **adjust** have? _____

2. Look at the pronunciation. Which letter is not pronounced, according to this dictionary? _____

3. Give one synonym for **adjust**. _____

4. What happens to some wild animals? _____

   _____

5. What sentence is given to illustrate the use of **adjust** in photography? _____

   _____

6. What is the adjective form of **adjust**? _____

7. What meaning do **adjust**, **adapt**, and **accommodate** have in common? _____

_____

READING

Fill-ins

Here are three reading passages. Five words are missing from each, as the numbered blanks show. After each passage is a list of seven words. From this list, choose the word that makes the best sense in each numbered blank.

A. Long, long ago, great forces were at work in the earth. In those

(1) _____ days rocks were formed and mountains were pushed up. The story of those days has not been lost to us. There is a(n)

(2) _____ of the changes left in the geology of the earth. For example, we know that part of what is now land was once under the sea. This is

shown by the fossils of (3) _____ animals and plants found in rocks. Scientists notice such things and through their careful

(4) _____ can see events of long ago. They can

(5) _____ into the murky history of the earliest times.

ancient   observation
marine   record
peer   solitary
tradition

B. Who are the latest brave explorers? The astronauts are the brave, even

(1) _____ heroes of today. Past explorers studied the far and unknown places of the earth. The astronauts carry on their

(2) _____ in outer space. In their strange outfits, they have

walked on the surface of the moon. The same (3) _____ has permitted strolls outside their capsule in empty space. Their work has

added much to our (4) _____ knowledge in chemistry, physics, and biology. We can look forward to even more in the future. We can

(5) _____ the time when space explorers will travel much farther out than they do today.

anticipate   intrepid
attire   investigation
harmony   oriental
scientific

C. One of the things we are curious about is whether there are forms of life in outer space. This life may be in animal form or in the form of

(1) _____ . It may be easily seen by the unaided eye or be

so small as to be visible only under the (2) _____ . In this
search, the astronauts carry with them all sorts of implements and instruments.

Some of this (3) _____ is sturdy but some is quite

(4) _____ . It would be a mighty serious event if
we do bump into a real space "alien." What will our feelings be on that

(5) _____ occasion?

apparatus	picnic
fragile	recreation
microscope	solemn

vegetation

TEST YOURSELF

From Column II select the best definition of each word in Column I. Write the letter for the definition in the space next to each word.

I

A

	I		II
_____	1. ceremony	a.	having to do with water
_____	2. aquatic	b.	special set of acts for special occasions
_____	3. balmy	c.	breathe out
_____	4. laboratory	d.	gentle
_____	5. exhale	e.	place for scientific work

B

_____	1. recreation	a.	amount of light
_____	2. edible	b.	decoration
_____	3. illumination	c.	alone
_____	4. ornament	d.	play
_____	5. solitary	e.	fit to eat

C

_____	1. peer	a.	eastern
_____	2. diligently	b.	agreement
_____	3. oriental	c.	look closely
_____	4. harmony	d.	serious
_____	5. solemn	e.	done in a hardworking manner.

D

_____	1. ancient	a.	outing
_____	2. tradition	b.	free time
_____	3. leisure	c.	very old
_____	4. excursion	d.	come down
_____	5. descend	e.	customs from the past

LE//ON 9

LOOK AT THE PICTURE

What Did You See?

1. Where is this scene?

   _____

2. What holiday is coming up? How do you know?

   _____

   _____

3. What kind of merchandise do you think is being sold?

   _____

   _____

4. Name or describe at least three examples of this kind of merchandise.

_____

_____

_____

5. Is the store running any sales? What makes you think so?

_____

_____

6. Which lesson word names the kind of person you see?

_____

7. Give two lesson words that tell what most of the people are expected to do.

_____

PRONUNCIATION

Here are ten lesson words suggested by the picture. With the help of your teacher, pronounce each word.

accuracy   (ak′ yər ə sē)
budget   (buj′ it)
celebration   (sel′ ə brā′ shən)
chores   (chôrz)
consumer   (kən sü′ mər)
items   (ī′ təmz)
merchandise   (mėr′ chən dīz)
purchase   (pėr′ chəs)
select   (si lekt′)
variety   (və rī′ ə tē)

SPELLING

Be sure you know how to spell each word. Here are the words given in sentences. Letters are missing from each word. First put the missing letters where they belong. Then write each complete word in the space.

1. Exact correctness in simple arithmetic is
   necessary in everyday life. For example,
   such AC_ _ _R_ _CY is needed in counting
   your change and in checking on bills.   1. _____

2. Every family should have a planned BU __ G __ T. In that way, the family will know just how much can be spent and how much saved.

2. _____

3. Birthdays, anniversaries, and certain holidays are generally a time for family C __ __ __ BRATION. These occasions are marked by special meals and parties.

3. _____

4. Every household must attend to everyday little jobs. These CHO __ __ S include shopping, cleaning, and cooking.

4. _____

5. People who buy things should have some protection against cheating by sellers. For that reason we have C __ __ __ UMER protection laws.

5. _____

6. Before shopping, I always draw up a list of __ T __ MS needed. That way I am sure not to forget a single thing.

6. _____

7. Some stores specialize in a particular kind of goods to be sold. For instance, the MER __ __ __ ND __ __ E of one store may be electronic equipment, of another, paper goods and stationery.

7. _____

8. She saved her money to buy a new bike. It took six months before she had enough to make the P __ R __ H __ SE.

8. _____

9. Who would be chosen as the new president of the club? The members finally decided to S __ LE __ __ Peter.

9. _____

10. Some gardeners prefer to grow just a few kinds of plants. Others prefer to have a great VAR __ __ __ Y, such as roses, irises, daylilies, chrysanthemums, daisies, tulips, daffodils, and violets.

10. _____

How Do These Words Go With the Picture?

How well can you see the connection between each word and the picture? For as many words as you can, explain briefly how the word goes with the picture.

1. **accuracy** _____

2. **budget** _____

3. celebration   _____

4. chores   _____

5. consumer   _____

6. items   _____

7. merchandise   _____

8. purchase   _____

9. select   _____

10. variety   _____

CONTEXT CLUES

Here are ten passages. The lesson word that completes each passage has been left out. See if you can write the proper word in each blank. Look for helpful clues in the passage. If you are not absolutely sure, take a good guess.

1. I went into the store to buy six things. I could only _____ three because I didn't have enough money for the others.

2. Most bathrooms will have certain necessary objects on a shelf or in a holder. These _____ include toothbrush, toothpaste, comb, brush, and scissors.

3. He couldn't make up his mind. At first he was going to choose a blue jacket, then a brown one. Finally he decided to _____ a gray one.

4. My mother has a carefully planned _____. It tells her just how much must be spent on necessities each month, such as rent, electricity, and food, and how much is left over for unexpected expenses, such as doctor bills.

5. Some people like to shop in stores that specialize in a single type of goods for sale. Others prefer department stores, which offer a wide _____ of things.

6. If buyers of goods don't have much money to spend, sellers are in trouble. If the _____ is prosperous, the seller will do well.

7. Many people like to browse in hardware stores because of the interesting

kind of _____ that can be bought. For sale are all sorts
of tools, holders, brackets, paints, and fasteners.

8. Some routine jobs are indoors, such as dishwashing and dusting. Other

_____ are outdoors, such as grass mowing, car wash-
ing, and snow shoveling.

9. Robin Hood is remembered for his _____ with the bow
and arrow. He struck the target in exactly the right place every time.

10. Graduation is always a time for happy _____, with
parties, presents, and congratulations.

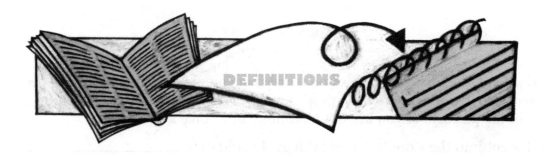

Most words have several meanings. Some words can be used as two or more
parts of speech. The Table shows one part of speech and one meaning for each
word. Study this information. After doing so, review your answers to Context
Clues. Correct any errors.

Word	Part of Speech	Definition
accuracy	noun	exactness; correctness; freedom from error
budget	noun	an estimate of the amount of money that will be received and spent for various purposes; a plan based on such an estimate
celebration	noun	the observation of a special occasion for joy, honor, or remembrance
chores	noun	small, everyday jobs or tasks
consumer	noun	a person who buys and uses any product
items	noun	separate things or articles
merchandise	noun	goods for sale; articles bought or sold; wares
purchase	verb	to get by paying a price; buy
select	verb	to pick out; choose
variety	noun	a number of different kinds; lack of sameness

Odd Word Out

One of the lesson words is shown in capital letters. It is followed by four other words or phrases. Three of these four belong closely with the capitalized word. Cross out the "stranger."

1. ACCURACY: arithmetic, carpentry, jogging, newspaper reporting
2. BUDGET: entertainment, household expenses, laughter, salary
3. CELEBRATION: birthday, graduation, homework, wedding
4. CHORES: dancing, dishwashing, laundry, dusting
5. MERCHANDISE: air, beverages, canned goods, vegetables

Headlines

Here is an imaginary newspaper headline. At least five of the lesson words are likely to appear in the article under the headline. List any three of these words. Then write one or two sentences including at least one of the three words you have chosen.

VAST NEW SHOPPING MALL TO OPEN

Words   _____   _____   _____

Sentences   _____

             _____

             _____

GRAMMAR

A. The words **budget, merchandise,** and **purchase** can be used as either nouns or verbs in a sentence. Tell whether the word in heavy type is a noun or a verb in each sentence.

1. The government **budgeted** the needed amount for repairs to roads and bridges.   1. _____

2. All governments have to prepare annual **budgets.**   2. _____

3. Paul earns money delivering newspapers, and he **budgets** a small amount for savings.   3. _____

4. The store has **merchandised** the personal computer so successfully that it is out of stock.   4. _____

5. The vegetable store **merchandises** only quality goods.   5. _____

6. The **merchandise** offered in the shop includes watches and calculators.

6. _____

7. What did you **purchase** on your shopping trip?

7. _____

8. My dad made many **purchases** with his bonus money.

8. _____

9. Lots of people are worried about the huge deficit in the Federal **budget.**

9. _____

B. The nouns **chores** and **items** are plurals. Write the singular of each.

_____ _____

Write the plural forms of these nouns.

1. celebration   _____

2. consumer   _____

3. purchase   _____

4. variety   _____

C. Form new words by following the directions. Then write the new words in the sentences.

1. Form an adjective from the noun **accuracy** by changing **cy** to **te.** _____

   A bank teller must be _____ in making the right change.

2. Form an adjective from the noun **budget** by adding the suffix **ary.** _____

   Nobody wanted to solve the _____ problems by raising taxes.

3. Form a verb from the noun **celebration.** _____

   Next week my grandfather will _____ his 80th birthday.

4. Form a verb from the noun **consumer.** _____

   American cars do not _____ as much fuel as they once did.

5. Form a noun from the verb **select.** _____

   The shop offered a wide _____ of shoe styles.

108   *Word Game*

WORDLORE

Anagrams

One word can be made into another by rearranging letters. Try these.

1. Rearrange the letters of ITEMS to mean what you can see on watches or clocks.

   1. _____

2. Rearrange the letters of ITEMS to form a word meaning "to hit" or "to strike."

   2. _____

3. Rearrange the letters of ITEMS to form a word meaning "gives off" or "sends out." This word would fit in the blank space of the sentence: The sun ___ light and heat.

   3. _____

4. Add an *r* to the rearranged letters of ITEMS to form a word meaning "deserves." This word would fit in the blank space of the sentence: Helen Keller ___ great admiration for dealing with her handicaps.

   4. _____

5. Can you add an *o* and an *n* to the rearranged letters of ITEMS to form a word meaning "to dampen" or "to make slightly wet"?

   5. _____

Try this. How many words of four or more letters can you form from the letters of MERCHANDISE? Try for ten. As a help, two are done for you.

dime	_____
cane	_____
_____	_____
_____	_____
_____	_____

Many English words begin with the prefix **con,** as in **consumer.** This prefix comes from a Latin word meaning "together" or "with." Write as many words as you can think of beginning with the prefix **con.** Do at least five. Can you do twenty?

_____	_____	_____	_____
_____	_____	_____	_____
_____	_____	_____	_____
_____	_____	_____	_____
_____	_____	_____	_____

Here is a reading passage that contains some of the lesson words. Read the passage. Then answer the questions that follow it.

In a few months, grandfather would be eighty years old. Everybody agreed we had to have a **celebration** to be attended by all the children, grandchildren, and great-grandchildren. So many people coming together from so many places would require a **variety** of plans.

First, a **budget** would have to be drawn up so that the expenses would not get out of hand. Then, the **chores** had to be divided. One person would **select** the gift. Another would plan the menu. A third would **purchase** the food.

Other **items** had to be attended to as well. Extra chairs and tables had to be rented. Someone had to become an informed **consumer** in that field and find a store that carried the most suitable **merchandise** of that type at the best price.

Father was in overall charge. His mission was to see to it that all plans were carried out with swiftness and **accuracy.**

1. What was the reason for planning the celebration?

   _____

2. Who would attend?

   _____

3. With so many attending, what would be required?

   _____

4. What would be done first?

   _____

5. What three chores are mentioned?

   _____

   _____

   _____

6. Why would someone have to become an informed consumer?

_____

_____

7. What was Father's mission?

_____

_____

WRITING

Write a short paragraph on the topic:

Running a family is like running a business.

Try to use at least three of the lesson words or their forms in your paragraph.

_____

_____

_____

_____

_____

_____

_____

ASSIGNMENT

See how many of the lesson words or forms of them you can find in newspapers, magazines, books, and other printed matter. If you find a word in newspapers or magazines that are ready to be thrown away, clip out the article or paragraph in which the word occurs. If you find any of the words in a book, copy the sentence in which the word appears. Then make a note of the title and author of the book. Your teacher will tell you when to bring your collection to class.

LESSON 10

What Did You See?

1. Where is this scene taking place?

   _____

2. What unusual thing is happening?

   _____

   _____

3. Why might this be frightening?

   _____

4. How does the person at the top of the picture appear to be feeling?

   _____

5. Who is the man walking beside the elephant?

   _____

   _____

6. Who are the other people?

   _____

   _____

PRONUNCIATION

Here are ten lesson words suggested by the picture. With the help of your teacher, pronounce each word.

> **adventurous**   (ad ven′ chər əs)
> **amble**   (am′ bəl)
> **domesticated**   (də mes′ tə kā tid)
> **elevation**   (el′ ə vā′ shən)
> **fee**   (fē)
> **gigantic**   (jī gan′ tik)
> **guide**   (gīd)
> **security**   (si kyủr′ ə tē)
> **sturdy**   (stėr′ dē)
> **timid**   (tim′ id)

SPELLING

Be sure you know how to spell each word. Here are the words given in sentences. Letters are missing from each word. First put the missing letters where they belong. Then write each complete word in the space.

1. Some people enjoy ADVEN__ __R__ __S activities, with a little danger in them, like downhill skiing or riding the rapids.

1. _____

2. People who are just out for a pleasure walk will __MB__E along slowly without a set direction.

2. _____

3. Some animals are wild, like the lion and the jaguar. Some are DOM__ __ __I__ATED, like sheep, goats, and cows.

3. _____

4. Planes ascend until they reach a cruising altitude. At that E__ __VAT__ __N, they level off.

4. _____

5. Children and senior citizens don't pay the same price as others do for movie tickets. They are charged a smaller admission F__ __.

5. _____

6. They are putting up a G__ __ __NTIC new building downtown. It will dwarf all the other buildings there now.

6. _____

7. Hansel and Gretel left a trail of bread crumbs behind them to act as a G__ __D__ to the way back out of the forest. The birds ate the crumbs!

7. _____

8. Seat belts are used as a safety measure in cars. The added SEC__ __ __TY they give will save many lives.

8. _____

9. The oak is a ST__ __D__ tree. Its deep roots, thick trunk, and hard wood make it strong.

9. _____

10. Some people fear nothing. Others are T__M__D about almost everything.

10. _____

How Do These Words Go With the Picture?

How well can you see the connection between each word and the picture? For as many words as you can, explain briefly how the word goes with the picture.

1. **adventurous** _____

2. **amble** _____

3. **domesticated** _____

4. **elevation** _____

5. **fee** _____

6. **gigantic** _____

7. **guide** _____

8. **security** _____

9. **sturdy** _____

10. **timid** _____

CONTEXT CLUES

Here are ten passages. The lesson word that completes each passage has been left out. See if you can write the proper word in each blank. Look for helpful clues in the passage. If you are not absolutely sure, take a good guess.

1. Dogs and cats are easily trained to become good house pets. Sometimes chimpanzees can also be _____ .

2. Some people seem to be naturally fearless and ready to try anything while others seem to be born _____ and are afraid of their own shadows.

3. Mount Everest is the highest peak in the world with an _____ of 29,028 feet.

4. Compared to the earth, the sun is enormous in size. It does not, however, look as _____ as it really is because it is so far away.

5. Safety is important in large school buildings, particularly against the danger of fire. Therefore, fire drills are conducted regularly for greater _____ .

6. On a beautiful spring day we went for a stroll in the park. It was pleasant to _____ along in a leisurely manner and enjoy the balmy weather and the blossoms.

7. The early explorers must have been _____ people who enjoyed the risks and excitement of traveling to far and unknown regions of the earth.

8. Every year the charge for riding on the bus goes up. Soon people won't be able to afford the _____ .

9. The weaker buildings were blown down in the tornado. Only those that were very _____ remained standing with very little damage.

10. Many tourists to foreign cities hire a _____ to lead the way to the most interesting sights. These escorts make it possible for the tourists to see more and learn more than they would on their own.

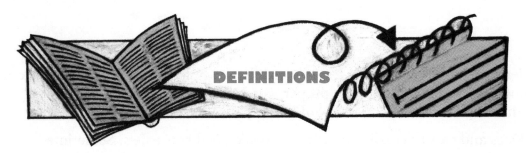

Most words have several meanings. Some words can be used as two or more parts of speech. The Table shows one part of speech and one meaning for each word. Study this information. After doing so, review your answers to Context Clues. Correct any errors.

Word	Part of Speech	Definition
adventurous	adjective	ready to take risks; daring
amble	verb	to walk at an easy, slow pace
domesticated	adjective	tamed; made part of human life
elevation	noun	height; altitude
fee	noun	the money charged for some service or activity; price of admission
gigantic	adjective	huge; enormous
guide	noun	a person who shows the way or leads or escorts
security	noun	safety; the feeling of being safe
sturdy	adjective	strong and firm
timid	adjective	easily frightened; fearful

THINKING

Word Quiz

Show how well you can use the words as part of your thinking. In the space, write the lesson word that best answers the question.

1. Which adjective best describes such animals as giraffes, whales, and elephants?

   1. _____

2. To what class of animals do cows, pigs, and horses belong that rattlesnakes, mountain lions, and wolves do not?

   2. _____

3. Which adjective best describes such animals as rabbits, mice, and deer?

   3. _____

4. What kinds of traits do jet pilots, trapeze artists, and mountain climbers have in common?

   4. _____

5. What do lawyers, doctors, and dentists get in return for their services?

   5. _____

6. A jack is used on a car having a flat tire. What is the main function of the jack?

   6. _____

7. What kind of walking are the following NOT likely to do: mail carriers, messengers, hikers, paraders?

   7. _____

8. How should houses be especially built in an area subject to frequent mild earthquakes?

   8. _____

9. What role does a seeing eye dog have for a blind person?

   9. _____

10. What is the function of doorlocks, guards, and fire extinguishers?

    10. _____

GRAMMAR

A. The words **amble** and **guide** can be used as either a noun or a verb. Tell whether the word in heavy type in each sentence is a noun or a verb.

1. Trail markers often serve as a **guide** to hikers.

   1. _____

2. In darkness, car drivers are often **guided** by the lights of the cars ahead.

   2. _____

3. Visitors to museums are often conducted around by **guides**.

   3. _____

4. Radar often **guides** the pilot of a plane or the captain of a ship.

   4. _____

5. My family used to go on **ambles** in the woods.   5. _____

6. The old horse **ambles** along as though there were all the
time in the world.   6. _____

7. The visitors **ambled** around the streets of the old village
taking in the sights.   7. _____

8. Don't **amble** along the way or you will be late.   8. _____

9. Buoys served as **guides** for safe entrance into the harbor. 9. _____

10. Nobody **ambles** who is in a hurry.   10. _____

B. Form new words by following the directions. Then write the new words
in the sentences.

1. Change **adventurous** to a noun by dropping the suffix **ous** and adding an **e**.

_____

Walking around in the big city was an _____ for
the country boy.

2. Change **sturdy** to a noun by changing the **y** to **i** and adding **ness**. _____

The oak tree is a symbol of _____ .

3. Change **elevation** to a verb. _____

The purpose of a jack is to _____ the car to change
a tire.

4. Change **security** to an adjective by dropping **ity** and adding an **e**. _____

People like to feel _____ in their own homes.

5. Change **timid** to a noun by adding **ity**. _____

Some actors, when off stage, show more _____ than
you might expect.

WORDLORE

Synonyms and Antonyms

Each lesson word is followed by two other words. One of those two words is
either a synonym or an antonym. Write the synonym or antonym in the first
space. Then write S or A to tell whether it is a synonym or antonym.

1. ADVENTUROUS: fearful, tell   _____ _____

2. AMBLE: talk, stroll   _____ _____

3. DOMESTICATED: tamed, sorry   _____ _____

4. ELEVATION: depth, hunger   _____ _____

5. FEE: food, charge   _____ _____

6. GIGANTIC: folded, tiny   _____ _____

7. GUIDE: leader, farmer   _____ _____

8. SECURITY: safety, use   _____ _____

9. STURDY: old, frail   _____ _____

10. TIMID: courageous, stormy   _____ _____

Write two sentences of your own. In the first, use one of the synonyms you have written. In the second, use one of the antonyms you have written.

1. _____

_____

2. _____

_____

Anagrams

One word can be made into another by rearranging the letters. Try these.

1. Rearrange the letters of AMBLE to form a word meaning "guilt" or "fault."   1._____

2. Add the letter G to AMBLE to form a word meaning "to take chances" or "to play games of chance."   2._____

3. Take the letter B out of AMBLE and rearrange the remaining letters to form a word that means the opposite of "female."   3._____

4. Rearrange the letters of the last word you formed to mean "walking with a limp."   4._____

5. Rearrange the letters of the last word you formed to mean "what is eaten three times a day."   5._____

READING COMPREHENSION

On the next page is a reading passage that contains some of the lesson words. Read the passage. Then answer the questions that follow it.

One summer, Richard went to work on a farm. The first day, the farmer told Richard to **amble** around the farm by himself to learn as much as he could. At dinner that night, Richard told the family what he had learned and was not **timid** about asking questions about what he did not understand. The second day the farmer's son acted as a **guide** and took Richard around to teach him more. As a last step, he led Richard to the top of a nearby hill that overlooked the farm. From that **elevation** Richard could see the whole layout.

In the days that followed Richard learned what hard and **adventurous** work it is to run a farm successfully. Crops and **domesticated** animals have to be protected from foxes, rabbits, coyotes, hawks, crows, and insects. He learned that measures for **security** included wired enclosures, fences, traps, dogs, and insecticides. Besides, the farmer has to worry about droughts and storms.

One day, the farmer's **gigantic** prize bull became very ill. The vet was called and treated the animal. The vet came every day for a week but the bull got sicker and sicker and died. To Richard's surprise, the vet charged no **fee** for his services because the animal had died. All the people who are involved in farm work are that way with each other, because the life is so hard and so uncertain.

It was quite a good summer's experience for Richard. He became a person more **sturdy** of both body and mind.

1. What did Richard do the first day on the farm?

   _____

   _____

2. How did Richard feel about asking questions? _____

3. What happened the second day?

   _____

   _____

4. What could Richard see from the elevation of the hill?

   _____

5. What kind of life is farm life?

   _____

6. What do foxes, rabbits, coyotes, hawks, crows, and insects threaten?

   _____

7. What are some security measures taken?

   _____

   _____

8. What happened to the gigantic prize bull?

   _____

9. Give one reason that the vet charged no fee.

   _____

10. What was the effect on Richard of the summer's experience?

   _____

WRITING

Write a short paragraph about a real or imaginary summer experience that you have had or that someone you know has had. Try to use at least three of the lesson words or forms of them in your paragraph.

    See how many of the lesson words or forms of them you can find in newspapers, magazines, books, and other printed matter. If you find a word in newspapers or magazines that are ready to be thrown away, clip out the article or paragraph in which the word occurs. If you find any of the words in a book, copy the sentence in which the word appears. Then make a note of the title and author of the book. Your teacher will tell you when to bring your collection to class.

LESSON 11

LOOK AT THE PICTURE

What Did You See?

1. What is the name of this sporting event?

   _____

2. What is the name of the leading horse?

   _____

3. What are the riders called?

   _____

4. Why do the riders wear goggles?

   _____

5. These riders are much smaller and lighter than most other athletes. Why?

_____

_____

6. What do the riders grasp in their hands? Why?

_____

7. Why do these races take place on an oval track rather than a straight one?

_____

_____

PRONUNCIATION

Here are ten lesson words suggested by the picture. With the help of your teacher, pronounce each word.

affirm   (ə fėrm′)
astride   (ə strīd′)
athletic   (ath let′ ik)
handicap   (han′ dē kap′)
headlong   (hed′ lông)
jubilation   (jü′ bə lā′ shən)
pace   (pās)
stamina   (stam′ ə nə)
tense   (tens)
triumph   (trī′ umf)

SPELLING

Be sure you know how to spell each word. Here are the words given in sentences. Letters are missing from each word. First put the missing letters where they belong. Then write each complete word in the space.

1. When presidents are sworn in, they AF__ __ __M their allegiance to the Constitution. This strong declaration is an important part of the ceremony.

1. _____

2. The older rider sat __STR__D__ the elephant. The small child, however, sat sideways, with both legs down one side.

2. _____

3. She was a very AT__ __ __TIC person, quick and strong in every sport.

3. _____

4. Midway in the game, the quarterback sprained his wrist. This HAN__ __ __AP made it difficult for him to throw the ball well.

4. _____

5. The speeding car went out of control and crashed H__ __DL__NG into the wall.

5. _____

6. When World War II ended, there was great joy. Crowds gathered in the streets expressing their J__ __ __LATION.

6. _____

7. The plumbers worked at great speed. This fast P__ __E enabled them to fix the leak in no time at all.

7. _____

8. Marathon runners need a lot of ST__ __ __NA. Otherwise, they would not have the power to last the distance.

8. _____

9. When the baby had to have his tonsils out, the family was very __ __NSE until the operation was over. When they heard everything had gone smoothly, they were able to relax.

9. _____

10. The TR__ __M__H of the home team in its final game came as a surprise. Nobody had expected the victory.

10. _____

How Do These Words Go With the Picture?

How well can you see the connection between each word and the picture? For as many words as you can, explain briefly how the word goes with the picture.

1. **affirm** _____

2. **astride** _____

3. **athletic** _____

4. **handicap** _____

5. **headlong** _____

6. **jubilation** _____

7. **pace** _____

8. stamina   _____

9. tense   _____

10. triumph   _____

CONTEXT CLUES

Here are ten passages. The lesson word that completes each passage has been left out. See if you can write the proper word in each blank. Look for helpful clues in the passage. If you are not absolutely sure, take a good guess.

1. Harold never rushed _____ into any job. Instead, he first thought it out and planned it carefully.

2. Pitching a no-hitter is the greatest victory any pitcher wants. It is a _____ that is rare.

3. The witnesses had to declare positively that they would tell the truth. They had to _____ that they would tell nothing but the truth.

4. The gymnast first sat _____ the balance beam; then she went into a handstand from which she came down with both legs together on one side of the bar.

5. It is not enough for a good racehorse to have speed. It must also have _____ or it will not have the lasting power to finish strong.

6. The mile race was run at a very fast _____ for the first three quarters. If that speed were kept up, the record would be broken.

7. The school had an all-around _____ program. It fielded teams in football, baseball, basketball, hockey, tennis, track, and lacrosse.

8. When George saw his excellent report card, his pleasure was great. His family also reacted with smiles of _____ .

9. Some people are relaxed and calm. Others are nervous and _____ .

10. To a football player, great size and weight are an advantage. To a jockey, they would be a _____ .

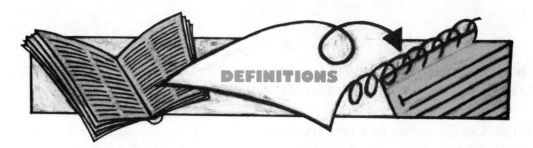

Most words have several meanings. Some words can be used as two or more parts of speech. The Table shows one part of speech and one meaning for each word. Study this information. After doing so, review your answers to Context Clues. Correct any errors.

Word	Part of Speech	Definition
affirm	verb	to say positively; declare solemnly; assure
astride	adverb	with a leg on either side; astraddle
athletic	adjective	having physical strength and skill, especially in sports
handicap	noun	a disadvantage; a race in which favorites are given a disadvantage (superior horses have to carry a greater weight)
headlong	adverb	headfirst; carelessly; recklessly
jubilation	noun	rejoicing; celebration
pace	noun	the rate of speed in walking or running; a step; type of step
stamina	noun	lasting power; endurance
tense	adjective	strained; nervous
triumph	noun	victory; success; achievement

THINKING

Sentence Sense

In each of the following sentences, one word does not make good sense. Cross it out and write a lesson word that will make the sentence sensible. Use the spaces to the right.

1. The quarterback was playing with the advantage of injured knees and a sprained shoulder. 1._____

2. The students were overjoyed by their team's loss in the state championships. 2._____

3. The crowd showed its sadness by cheering, singing, and dancing in the aisles. 3._____

4. Jack's outstanding musical ability assured his making the football, baseball, and basketball teams. 4._____

5. Cowboys and jockeys are more at home than most of us when they are without a horse. 5._____

Word Quiz

Show how well you can use the words as part of your thinking. In the space, write the lesson word that best answers the question.

1. What does the leader in a race try to set?   1._____
2. What is especially required for marathons, basketball, mountain climbing, and long-distance swimming?   2._____
3. How would a careless person rush across the street?   3._____
4. How do many people feel when they are about to take an important exam?   4._____
5. What do witnesses have to do about telling the truth before taking the stand in a court trial?   5._____

GRAMMAR

A. The words **handicap**, **pace**, and **triumph** can be used either as verbs or nouns in a sentence. Tell whether the word in heavy type is a verb or a noun.

1. Abraham Lincoln overcame hardships and **handicaps** to become President of the United States.   1. _____
2. Poverty and family tragedy were among his **handicaps**.   2. _____
3. My shyness **handicaps** me in many situations.   3. _____
4. A sore elbow **handicapped** the tennis star and she had to withdraw from the tournament.   4. _____
5. Window shoppers usually stroll along at a leisurely **pace**.   5. _____
6. The tiger **paced** back and forth in his cage.   6. _____
7. A nervous person often **paces** about without being able to sit still.   7. _____
8. The trot, the canter, and the gallop are three different **paces** of horses.   8. _____
9. Our team **triumphed** in the final game of the season.   9. _____
10. In the well-known fable, a tortoise **triumphs** over a hare in a race.   10. _____

B. Form new words by following the directions. Then write the new words in the sentences.

1. Change the verb **affirm** to a noun by adding **ation**. _____

   The audience cheered in _____ when the mayor proposed repairing the bridge.

128   *Word Game*

2. Change **tense** to a noun by dropping the final **e** and adding **ion**. _____

    You could almost feel the _____ in the room just before the rocket launching.

3. Change **athletic** to a noun by dropping the **ic** and adding an **e**. _____

    She was an all-around _____ .

4. Write the plural of the word you formed in 3. _____

    _____ have to train hard to be successful.

5. Change **triumph** to an adjective by adding **ant**. _____

    Tarzan let out a _____ yell.

6. Write the plural of the noun **pace**. _____

    Horses are trained in different _____ , such as trot, canter, and gallop.

7. Write the past tense of the verb **pace**. _____

    The lion _____ back and forth.

8. Write the past tense of the verb **handicap**. First add another **p**; then add **ed**.

    _____

    Polio _____ Franklin Roosevelt, but it did not stop him.

9. Write the plural of the noun **handicap**. _____

    One way or another, _____ can be overcome.

10. Write the plural of the noun **triumph**. _____

    The _____ of Napoleon came to an end in Russia.

Choose any two of the new words you have formed and write them in sentences of your own.

1. _____

    _____

2. _____

    _____

WORDLORE

Synonyms

In Column I are seven of the lesson words. In Column II are synonyms of the words. Match up the words and synonyms by writing the proper synonym in the space alongside each lesson word.

<table>
<tr><td></td><td>I</td><td>II</td></tr>
<tr><td>_____</td><td>1. handicap</td><td>nervous</td></tr>
<tr><td>_____</td><td>2. headlong</td><td>joy</td></tr>
<tr><td>_____</td><td>3. jubilation</td><td>disadvantage</td></tr>
<tr><td>_____</td><td>4. pace</td><td>victory</td></tr>
<tr><td>_____</td><td>5. stamina</td><td>recklessly</td></tr>
<tr><td>_____</td><td>6. tense</td><td>speed</td></tr>
<tr><td>_____</td><td>7. triumph</td><td>endurance</td></tr>
</table>

Choose any two of the synonyms you have written and write each in a sentence of your own.

1. _____

_____

2. _____

_____

The Dictionary

tense¹ (tens), *adj.*, tens er, tens est, *v.*, tensed, tens ing. —*adj.*
1 stretched tight; strained to stiffness: *a tense rope, a face tense with pain.* 2 keyed up; strained: *tense nerves, a tense moment.* 3 (in phonetics) pronounced with the muscles of the speech organs relatively tense. —*v.t., v.i.* stretch tight; tighten; stiffen: *I tensed my muscles for the leap.* [< Latin *tensum* < *tendere* to stretch] —tense' ly, *adv.* —tense' ness, *n.*
tense² (tens), *n.* 1 form of a verb that shows the time of the action or state expressed by the verb. *I dance* is in the present tense. *I danced* is in the past tense. *I will dance* is in the future tense. 2 set of such forms for the various persons. [< Old French *tens* time < Latin *tempus.* Doublet of TEMPO] —tense' less, *adj.*

1. What is the word for "more tense"? For "most tense"?

_____ _____

2. When **tense** means "stretched tight," what two examples of tense things are given?

   _____   _____

3. When **tense** means "keyed up," what two examples of tense things are given?

   _____   _____

4. You are told that **tense** can be two different parts of speech. Circle the names of those parts of speech from the following:

   noun   adjective   verb   pronoun

5. In the first entry, what is the meaning of the Latin words from which **tense** comes?

   _____

6. Why is there a separate second entry for **tense**?

   _____

7. What is the meaning of **tense** in the second entry?

   _____

8. What is the meaning of the Old French word from which this **tense** comes?

   _____

9. What is the tense of "He obeys"? _____

10. What is the tense of "He will obey"? _____

READING COMPREHENSION

Here is a reading passage that contains some of the lesson words. Read the passage. Then answer the questions that follow it.

The Olympic Games started in ancient Greece. These games were held every four years in honor of the god Zeus. At that time, the separate Greek states were often at war. To honor Zeus during the game, there was a truce. Besides, the competitors had to **affirm** that their names were free from dishonor.

In the earliest Olympics, the only **athletic** events were footraces. Later, wrestling, boxing, jumping, and discus throwing were added. There was also a form of horse racing but the riders did not sit **astride** their horses. Instead, they stood in small chariots and drove the horses in a furious, **headlong** rush.

The most prized event was the pentathlon, which consisted of five different sports and was regarded as the supreme test of skill, strength, and **stamina.**

Triumph in the Olympics was rewarded with many great honors. The winners were crowned with wreaths of the sacred olive. Stories and poems were dedicated to them.

The modern Olympics are like the ancient ones in some ways. The competition is very **tense.** Victories are celebrated with awards, ceremonies, and **jubilation.** The modern Olympics are also different in many ways. Today, there is even an Olympics for people with a **handicap.**

If you think about the ancient and modern Olympics, you may wonder about two questions. Could those ancient runners have kept **pace** with modern ones? Are the modern Olympics true to the great ideals of the ancient ones?

1. Name two ways the ancient Olympics showed honor to Zeus.

   _____

   _____

2. What were the only athletic events in the first Olympics?

   _____

3. Where were the riders in the horse races?

   _____

4. How did they drive the horses?

   _____

5. What position did the pentathlon have?

   _____

6. Name two ways in which the ancient Olympics were like the modern ones.

_____

_____

7. What two questions may someone who thinks about the Olympics wonder about?

_____

_____

_____

_____

WRITING

Write a short paragraph suggested to your mind by any one of the following lesson words:

JUBILATION   TRIUMPH   TENSE   HANDICAP

_____

_____

_____

_____

_____

_____

_____

_____

ASSIGNMENT

See how many of the lesson words or forms of them you can find in newspapers, magazines, books, and other printed matter. If you find a word in newspapers or magazines that are ready to be thrown away, clip out the article or paragraph in which the word occurs. If you find any of the words in a book, copy the sentence in which the word appears. Then make a note of the title and author of the book. Your teacher will tell you when to bring your collection to class.

LESSON 12

LOOK AT THE PICTURE

What Did You See?

1. What kind of boat are these people probably on? Why?

_____

_____

2. What is the man on the left, as well as others, probably doing?

_____

3. What time of year is this? How do you know?

_____

_____

4. What are the probable feelings of these people?

_____

5. What will some of the people probably do when they get to their destination?

_____

6. Name two other places or sights that people such as these visit in large numbers.

_____

_____

PRONUNCIATION

Here are ten lesson words suggested by the picture. With the help of your teacher, pronounce each word.

aloft   (ə lôft′)
ascend   (ə send′)
convey   (kən vā′)
heritage   (her′ ə tij)
immigrant   (im′ ə grənt)
inspire   (in spīr′)
monument   (mon′ yə mənt)
refuge   (ref′ yüj)
symbol   (sim′ bəl)
tourists   (tùr′ ists)

SPELLING

Be sure you know how to spell each word. Here are the words given in sentences. Letters are missing from each word. First put the missing letters where they belong. Then write each complete word in the space.

1. A hawk was soaring A__ __FT, searching the ground far below for sight of a rabbit or other prey.

1. _____

2. We watched the hawk A__ __END even higher on currents of air that helped carry it up.

2. _____

3. Some people use buses to CONV__ __ them to work. The train carries many others.

3. _____

4. The greatest H_ _ _ _T_GE that has been handed down to Americans from those who founded the country is belief in democracy and the freedom of thought that goes with it.

4. _____

5. His father came to settle here as an I_ _ _ _GR_NT from Europe seeking greater opportunity.

5. _____

6. Education is meant to _NSP_ _E us with a love of truth and knowledge. Yet, there are some people who are uplifted by that feeling even without education.

6. _____

7. The faces of four presidents have been carved in the stone of Mount Rushmore as a lasting M_N_M_NT of their greatness.

7. _____

8. When the tornado alert was announced, many people sought REF_ _E in the firehouse, for they did not feel their homes were safe places.

8. _____

9. The dove is a S_MB_L of peace, while the eagle stands for strength.

9. _____

10. Among the places that T_ _R_STS come to in great numbers are Grand Canyon, Gettysburg, and New Orleans. These visiting travelers like to see historic or otherwise interesting places.

10. _____

How Do These Words Go With the Picture?

How well can you see the connection between each word and the picture? For as many words as you can, explain briefly how the word goes with the picture.

1. **aloft** _____

2. **ascend** _____

3. **convey** _____

4. **heritage** _____

5. **immigrant** _____

6. **inspire** _____

7. **monument** _____

8. **refuge** _____

9. **symbol** _____

10. **tourists** _____

CONTEXT CLUES

Here are ten passages. The lesson word that completes each passage has been left out. See if you can write the proper word in each blank. Look for helpful clues in the passage. If you are not absolutely sure, take a good guess.

1. In the old days of sailing ships, sailors had to be skilled at climbing _____ to the tops of the tall masts.

2. Modern Italy has a tradition from its past of great art, architecture, and music. This _____ makes Italy a proud country.

3. Every summer Italy is crowded with visitors from all over the world. These _____ flock to see its ancient buildings and museums.

4. Many snakes do no harm and some are even beneficial. Yet, instead of standing for good, the snake is a _____ of evil.

5. How is freight shipped around the country? Mainly, either trucks or trains _____ it.

6. We used the elevator to _____ to the fifth floor and we descended on the escalator.

7. Colorful sunsets and starry nights _____ us with appreciation of the beauties of nature.

8. If there is lightning, it is unwise to seek _____ from rainfall under a tree. There is not safety but danger there.

9. The Lincoln Memorial in Washington, D.C., is a beautiful structure. It is a _____ dedicated to the memory of a great man.

10. Albert Einstein came to live in America as an _____ from Germany. This newcomer to our country became one of its greatest citizens.

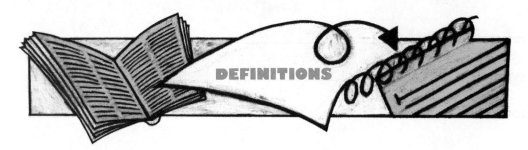

Most words have several meanings. Some words can be used as two or more parts of speech. The Table shows one part of speech and one meaning for each word. Study this information. After doing so, review your answers to Context Clues. Correct any errors.

Word	Part of Speech	Definition
aloft	adverb	high up; in the air
ascend	verb	to go up; rise; move upward
convey	verb	to take from one place to another; carry; transport
heritage	noun	something handed down from the past
immigrant	noun	a person who goes from one country to another to live
inspire	verb	to move towards some creative effort or act; fill with some feeling or thought; influence
monument	noun	something set up to keep alive the memory of a person or event, as a tablet, statue, or building
refuge	noun	a place of safety or shelter
symbol	noun	a particular object that stands for an idea or feeling
tourists	noun	people who go on a trip for sightseeing and pleasure

THINKING

Word Quiz

1. Give two lesson words that have something directly to do with movement or motion.

   _____   _____

2. Give a word that has something directly to do with escaping from danger, discomfort, or inconvenience.

   _____

3. Give two words that have something directly to do with remembering the past.

   _____   _____

4. Give two words that name people on the move.

   _____   _____

5. What class of things does the flag belong to?

   _____

Odd Word Out

One of the list words is shown in capital letters. It is followed by four other words. Three of these words belong with the capitalized word. One does not. Cross out the "stranger."

1. ALOFT: bird, kite, plane, tunnel

2. ASCEND: elevator, escalator, parachute, stairs

3. CONVEY: rain, ship, train, truck

4. HERITAGE: customs, weather, ideals, language

5. TOURISTS: camera, guide, kitchen, suitcase

Sentence Sense

In each of the following sentences, one word does not make good sense. Cross it out and write a lesson word that will make the sentence sensible. Use the spaces to the right.

1. When families move, they usually have to hire a large truck to polish their belongings from their old home to their new one.   1._____

2. The mountain climber was now far below, near the peak, where the air was thin and breathing was difficult.   2._____

3. A red flag is often used as a floor of danger.   3._____

4. Native Americans are proud of their rocks as friends of the environment.   4._____

5. Many gardeners visit the pyramids of Egypt, listening to the guides and taking photos.   5._____

GRAMMAR

A. Form new words by following the directions. Then write the new words in the sentences.

1. Change the verb **ascend** to a noun meaning "the act of going up", by changing the **d** to a **t**. _____

    The first _____ in a balloon occurred long ago.

2. Form the past tense of **convey** by adding **ed**. _____

    The prospectors _____ their belongings on the backs of mules.

3. Change the verb **convey** to a noun meaning "something used to convey" by adding the suffix **ance**. _____

    The covered wagon is a historic _____ .

4. Form the plural of **immigrant**. _____

    Many _____ come from Asia.

5. Change the noun **immigrant** to a verb by substituting **ate** for **ant**.

    _____

    People _____ for many different reasons.

6. An **immigrant** is someone who comes to a foreign country. Form a word meaning "someone who leaves his or her own country" by substituting **em** for **imm**. _____

    During the revolution, many of the French nobility were

    _____ s to England.

7. Change the verb **inspire** to a noun by dropping the final **e** and adding **ation**.

    _____

    The flag is an _____ to many people.

8. Change the word you formed in 7 to an adjective by adding the suffix **al**.

    _____

    John Philip Sousa wrote _____ music.

9. Change the noun **monument** to an adjective by adding the suffix **al**.

    _____

    The signing of the peace treaty was a _____ occasion.

10. Change **refuge** to another noun meaning "someone who is seeking refuge" by adding another e after the last e. _____

_____ s from tyranny flocked to America.

B.

> The suffix **ist** can be added to words to form a noun. The suffix **ist** means "a person who does or performs or a person who is an expert in." For example, the word **tour** + the suffix **ist** forms a word meaning "a person who tours."

Add the suffix **ist** to the following words to form new words.

1.   art + ist = _____
2.   violin + ist = _____
3.   humor + ist = _____
4. cartoon + ist = _____
5. journal + ist = _____

> The suffix **ant** also means "a person who does or performs."

Add the suffix **ant** to the following words to form new words.

6.   assist + ant = _____
7. account + ant = _____
8.   defend + ant = _____

> The suffixes **er** and **or** also mean "a person who does or performs."

Add **er** or **or** to the following words to form new words.

9.   act + or = _____
10.   speak + er = _____
11.   follow + er = _____
12.   lead + er = _____
13. invent + or = _____
14. mourn + er = _____
15. govern + or = _____

Synonyms and Antonyms

Find a word in Column II that is either a synonym or an antonym of each word in Column I and write it in the space. In the second space, tell whether it is a synonym or antonym, using S or A.

			I	II
_____	_____	1.	aloft	memorial
_____	_____	2.	ascend	below
_____	_____	3.	convey	emigrant
_____	_____	4.	heritage	sightseers
_____	_____	5.	immigrant	descend
_____	_____	6.	monument	carry
_____	_____	7.	refuge	inheritance
_____	_____	8.	tourists	safety

Choose any two of the words you have written and use each in a sentence of your own.

1. _____

_____

2. _____

_____

Rhymes

Have some fun with rhymes. Select the lesson word to complete each of the following rhymes.

1. Give a thought to the meaning of "thimble."

   Of anything small it is often a _____.

2. To push the "down" button we did intend;

   The elevator then began to _____.

3. When we went out, the breeze was so soft,

   Our kite was aground instead of _____.

4. Thomas Jefferson in the nation entire

   A deep love of freedom did _____.

5. Some trains carry travelers along their way.

While others will only some freight _____.

The Dictionary

Here is the dictionary entry for **symbol**. Read the entry. Then, answer the questions.

> **symbol** (sim′ bəl), n., v., **-boled**, **-bol ing** or **-bolled**, **-bol ling**. —*n.*
> 1 something that stands for or represents an idea, quality, condi-
> tion, or other abstraction: *The lion is the symbol of courage; the
> lamb, of meekness; the olive branch, of peace; the cross, of Chris-
> tianity.* See **emblem** for synonym study. 2 letter, figure, or sign con-
> ventionally standing for some object, process, etc.: *The letters Hg
> are the symbol for the chemical element mercury. The marks +, −,
> ×, and ÷ are symbols for add, subtract, multiply, and divide.* —
> *v.t.* **symbolize.** [< Greek *symbolon* token, mark < *syn-*together +
> *ballein* to throw]

1. Give three examples of things that stand for an "idea, quality, condition, or other abstraction."

   _____   _____   _____

2. To what word are you referred for synonym study?

   _____

3. Give two examples of letters or figures used as symbols.

   _____   _____

4. What verb can be formed from the noun **symbol**?

   _____

5. From what ancient language does **symbol** come?

   _____

6. What are the English meanings in that language for **syn** and **ballein**?

   _____   _____

READING COMPREHENSION

Here is a reading passage that contains some of the lesson words. Read the passage. Then answer the questions that follow it.

The great national parks of the Far West are among the richest treasures of our nation. Of these parks, the most spectacular and popular is Yosemite.

Yosemite is important as a **refuge** for many, many kinds of wildlife. Yosemite is important for the many awesome natural wonders, such as Half-Dome and Bridal Veil Falls, that **inspire tourists** with appreciation of nature.

In the summer, vehicles of every type **convey** to the park many hundreds of thousands of visitors. These visitors **ascend** the heights of the great mountains that rise to an elevation of over two miles. They explore the beautiful valleys that have been carved by the Merced and Tuolumne Rivers. They watch for the deer and the bears that thrive in this wilderness and for the eagle— the **symbol** of strength—that soars **aloft**. The visitor to Yosemite can be compared to an emigrant seeking to escape the pollution and ugliness of civilization to live, at least for a short while, in the clean air and unspoiled environment of nature.

Our national parks, such as Yosemite, can be regarded as a natural **monument** to those who have had the foresight to protect the best in our environment and as a key part of the precious **heritage** of all Americans.

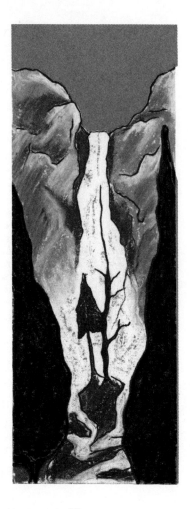

1. What are among the richest treasures of our nation?

   _____

2. How does Yosemite stand among these? _____

   _____

3. Give two ways in which Yosemite is important. _____

   _____

   _____

4. How many visitors are conveyed to the park every year?

   _____

5. Name two things the visitors do. _____

   _____

   _____

6. What symbol is mentioned? _____

_____

7. To what can the visitor be compared? _____

_____

_____

8. Give two ways that our national parks should be regarded.

_____

_____

WRITING

Write a short paragraph about a time when you or someone you know or someone you have learned about through reading or television viewing has been either **a tourist** or an **immigrant**. Try to use at least three of the lesson words or forms of them in your paragraph.

_____

_____

_____

_____

_____

_____

_____

ASSIGNMENT

See how many of the lesson words or forms of them you can find in newspapers, magazines, books, and other printed matter. If you find a word in newspapers or magazines that are ready to be thrown away, clip out the articles or paragraphs in which the word occurs. If you find any of the words in a book, copy the sentence in which the word appears. Then make a note of the title and author of the book. Your teacher will tell you when to bring your collection to class.

REVIEW
LESSONS 9-12

LOOK AT THE PICTURE

What Did You See?

1. What kind of place is this?

_____

2. What time of year is it?

_____

3. What part of the workday does it seem to be? How do you know?

_____

_____

4. What kinds of work do you think the people do?

_____

_____

5. Besides cars, trucks, taxis, and buses, what other vehicle is provided for? How do you know?

_____

_____

Here are the forty words you have learned so much about in Lessons 9-12. First review the list by saying each word aloud. Then go on to the review exercises and refer to this list as you need to.

accuracy	adventurous	affirm	aloft
budget	amble	astride	ascend
celebration	domesticated	athletic	convey
chores	elevation	handicap	heritage
consumer	fee	headlong	immigrant
items	gigantic	jubilation	inspire
merchandise	guide	pace	monument
purchase	security	stamina	refuge
select	sturdy	tense	symbol
variety	timid	triumph	tourist

How Do These Words Go With the Picture?

Here are three lesson words. Briefly explain the connection of each to the picture.

1. **gigantic** _____

2. **consumer** _____

3. **amble** _____

Now select from the review list five other lesson words that you feel are connected to the picture. Write each word and briefly explain the connection.

_____   _____

_____   _____

_____   _____

_____   _____

_____   _____

Ideas

You are given words suggesting a general idea. For each, select three lesson words that are closely connected with the idea. Write the words. Then choose one word and write it in a sentence of your own.

1. MONEY

   Words: _____ _____ _____

   Sentence: _____

   _____

2. TRAVEL

   Words: _____ _____ _____

   Sentence: _____

   _____

3. PEOPLE

   Words: _____ _____ _____

   Sentence: _____

   _____

4. HOPE

   Words: _____ _____ _____

   Sentence: _____

   _____

Scrambled Words and Anagrams

Here are five lesson words with the letters scrambled. On line **a**, write the word with the letters in the correct order. On line **b**, follow the instructions for each word.

1. CEPA   a._____

   Add *H* to the letters of your word and use those letters to form a word meaning "costing very little."   b._____

2. SENET   a._____

   Add *R* to the letters of your word and use those letters to form a word meaning "goes in."   b._____

3. BLEAM   a._____

   Add *R* to the letters of your word and use those letters to form a word meaning "a hard stone, usually
   white, used in buildings and sculpture."   b._____

4. LECSET

a._____

Add *A* and *N* to the letters of your word and use those letters to form a word meaning "least dirty."

b._____

5. ETIMS

a._____

Add *N* and *U* to the letters of your word and use those letters to form a new word meaning "units of time consisting of sixty seconds."

b._____

GRAMMAR

A. Write the plurals of these nouns.

1. budget   _____

2. celebration   _____

3. fee   _____

4. guide   _____

5. symbol   _____

Use any one of the words you have written in a sentence of your own.

_____

_____

B. Change each word to a verb that will fit sensibly when you write it in the blank space in each sentence.

1. **celebration**

Many families _____ Thanksgiving with a dinner.

2. **consumer**

We watched the chimp _____ three bananas.

3. **elevation**

A forklift truck can _____ a heavy load from the street to the truck bed.

Use any of the words you have written in a sentence of your own.

_____

_____

C. Change each word to a noun that will fit sensibly when you write it in the blank space in each sentence.

1. **select**

    In the winter there was a poor _____ of fruits available.

2. **affirm**

    The senate voted in _____ of the resolution.

3. **inspire**

    Madame Curie's husband was an _____ to her.

Use any one of the words you have written in a sentence of your own.

_____

_____

D. Write the past tense of these verbs.

1. purchase   _____

2. select   _____

3. amble   _____

4. affirm   _____

5. convey   _____

Use any one of the words you have written in a sentence of your own.

_____

_____

The Dictionary

Here is the dictionary entry for **inspire**. Look it over. Answer the questions.

in spire (in spīr′), *v.*, **-spired, -spir ing.** —*v.t.* **1** fill with a thought or feeling; influence: *A chance to try again inspired him with hope.* **2** cause (thought or feeling): *The leader's courage inspired confidence in the others.* **3** put thought, feeling, life, force, etc., into: *The speaker inspired the crowd.* **4** cause to be told or written: *His enemies inspired false stories about him.* **5** arouse or influence by a divine force. **6** breathe in; inhale. —*v.i.* breathe in air. [< Latin *inspirare* < *in-* in + *spirare* breathe] —**in spir′a ble,** *adj.* —**in spir′er,** *n.* —**in spir′ing ly,** *adv.*

1. What are the two syllables into which **inspire** can be divided? _____

2. What is the meaning of the Latin root from which the second syllable comes?

   _____

3. The prefix **con** means "together." What is the original meaning of the word **conspire?**

   _____

4. What sentence is given to illustrate the meaning "cause thought or feeling?"

   _____

   _____

5. Notice the last meaning of **inspire**, "breathe in air." Can you guess what word would mean exactly the opposite? (Hint: The prefix **ex** means the opposite of **in.**)

   _____

6. What adverb can be formed from **inspire?**

   _____

READING

Fill-ins

Here are three reading passages. Five words are missing from each, as the numbered blanks show. After each passage is a list of seven words. From this list, choose the word that makes the best sense in each blank space.

A. Americans have always gone to Europe to visit, but once you could

hardly find a European (1) _____ visiting here. That has

changed. Many Europeans plan their (2) _____ to have
enough money for a trip to America. A few come by ship but most prefer to have

jumbo jets (3) _____ them across the Atlantic. Their first

view of America is not from the ground but from (4) _____

through the windows of the plane. It is an exciting, (5) _____
moment for them as they prepare to land.

accuracy	chores
aloft	convey
budget	tourist
tense	

B. On both sides of the Atlantic, tourists are alike in many ways. They will spend part of a day visiting a museum or an important building or some (1) _____ of the past. They will spend the rest of a day in the shops seeking to (2) _____ items for themselves or as presents for others. They will do as much walking about as their staying power permits. When their (3) _____ begins to run out, they will (4) _____along much more slowly. Soon they are totally exhausted and are ready to pay the (5) _____ for a train, bus, or taxi rather than walk.

amble	fee
athletic	monument
astride	purchase
	stamina

C. Most of the people who have come to America from overseas have not come as tourists. Most have come as (1) _____ to make this country their permanent home. Why did they come? Some came to seek (2) _____from the danger of oppression, poverty, and war. They came because they wanted to share in the (3) _____ Americans have from their past of freedom and equality. The Statue of Liberty, a (4) _____of those traditions, was the first sight many of the newcomers saw. Some came because they were curious and restless. They were brave and (5) _____people who sought the excitement and variety of the new land.

adventurous	heritage
domesticated	immigrants
elevation	refuge
	symbol

TEST YOURSELF

From Column II select the best definition of each word in Column I. Write the letter for the definition in the space next to the word.

I		**II**

A

_____ 1. accuracy

_____ 2. affirm

_____ 3. amble

_____ 4. astride

_____ 5. celebration

a. walk slowly

b. correctness; exactness

c. observation of a special occasion

d. declare positively

e. sitting with the legs on either side

B

_____ 1. domesticated

_____ 2. convey

_____ 3. handicap

_____ 4. jubilation

_____ 5. inspire

a. carry

b. fill with a strong feeling

c. tamed; trained; not wild

d. disadvantage

e. great joy

C

_____ 1. consumer

_____ 2. headlong

_____ 3. merchandise

_____ 4. pace

_____ 5. monument

a. with speed and force

b. a memorial structure

c. rate of speed

d. person who uses goods and services

e. goods for sale

D

_____ 1. security

_____ 2. refuge

_____ 3. sturdy

_____ 4. timid

_____ 5. triumph

a. strong and solid

b. easily frightened

c. place of safety

d. victory

e. safety

(Numbers in parentheses indicate lessons.)

_____ **A** _____

accuracy (ak′ yər ə sē) *n.* exactness; correctness; freedom from error   (9)

adjust (ə just′) *v.* to change or rearrange something to make it more suitable   (5)

adventurous (ad ven′ chər əs) *adj.* ready to take risks; daring   (10)

affection (ə fek′ shən) *n.* warm feeling; fondness; love   (1)

affirm (ə fėrm′) *v.* to say positively; declare solemnly; assure   (11)

agriculture (ag′ rə kul′ chər) *n.* farming; the science and art of producing crops and raising livestock   (2)

aide (ād) *n.* helper; assistant   (3)

aloft (ə lôft′) *adv.* high up; in the air   (12)

amble (am′ bəl) *v.* to walk at an easy, slow pace   (10)

ancient (ān′ shənt) *adj.* belonging to times long past; very old   (6)

anticipate (an tis′ ə pāt) *v.* to expect; to look forward to   (8)

apparatus (ap′ ə rat′ əs) *n.* tools, machinery, or other equipment for a particular use   (7)

aquatic (ə kwôt′ ik) *adj.* having to do with water   (7)

ascend (ə send′) *v.* to go up; rise; move upward   (12)

astride (ə strīd′) *adv.* with a leg on either side; astraddle   (11)

athletic (ath let′ ik) *adj.* having physical strength and skill, especially in sports   (11)

attendant (ə ten′ dənt) *n.* a person who serves or looks after things   (3)

attire (ə tīr′) *n.* clothing; the way a person is dressed   (6)

_____ **B** _____

balmy (bä′ mē) *adj.* mild; gentle; soothing; pleasant   (8)

budget (buj′ it) *n.* an estimate of the amount of money that will be received and spent for various purposes; a plan used on such an estimate   (9)

_____ **C** _____

celebration (sel′ ə brā′ shən) *n.* the observation of a special occasion for joy, honor, or remembrance   (9)

ceremony (ser′ ə mō′ nē) *n.* a special set of acts for special occasions, such as weddings, graduations, and inaugurations   (6)

chores (chôrz) *n.* small, everyday jobs or tasks   (9)

companionship (kəm pan′ yən ship) *n.* fellowship; comradeship; company   (8)

concentrate (kon′ sən trāt) *v.* to pay close attention; focus the mind on   (4)

construction (kən struk′ shən) *n.* act of building; act of putting together   (4)

consumer (kən sü′ mər) *n.* a person who buys and uses any product   (9)

contrast (kon′ trast) *n.* sharp difference between things or people being compared   (2)

convey (kən vā′) *v.* to take from one place to another; carry; transport   (12)

craft (kraft) *n.* a trade or kind of work requiring special skill or ability   (4)

cultivate (kul′ tə vāt) *v.* to prepare and improve land for growing crops   (2)

─────────── **D** ───────────

departure (di pär′ chər) *n.* leaving; going away   (3)

descend (di send′) *v.* to go or come down   (7)

diligently (dil′ ə jənt lē) *adv.* done in a hardworking, industrious manner   (5)

dispute (dis pyüt′) *n.* argument; quarrel; disagreement   (1)

domesticated (də mes′ tə kā tid) *adj.* tamed; made part of human life   (10)

drought (drout) *n.* absence of rainfall or snow for a long time; a dry spell   (2)

dwelling (dwel′ ing) *n.* place in which one lives; house; residence   (4)

─────────── **E** ───────────

edible (ed′ ə bəl) *adj.* fit to eat   (7)

elevation (el′ ə vā′ shən) *n.* height; altitude   (10)

escape (e skāp′) *v.* to get away from; get free from   (8)

excursion (ek skėr′ zhən) *n.* a short journey or trip, often taken by a number of people together   (8)

exhale (eks hāl′) *v.* to breathe out   (7)

extension (ek sten′ shən) *n.* something added, such as a room or a length of wire   (4)

─────────── **F** ───────────

fee (fē) *n.* money charged for some service or activity; price of admission   (10)

fertile (fėr′ tl) *adj.* able to produce richly   (2)

foliage (fō′ lē ij) *n.* leaves of a plant or tree   (2)

fragile (fraj′ əl) *adj.* easily broken or damaged; frail; delicate   (6)

function (fungk′ shən) *n.* use or purpose   (4)

─────────── **G** ───────────

gesture (jes′ chər) *n.* a movement or sign of any part of the body to express a meaning; signal; motion   (1)

gigantic (jī gan′ tik) *adj.* huge; enormous   (10)

grasp (grasp) *n.* a firm hold with the hand; grip   (1)

guide (gīd) *n.* a person who shows the way or leads or escorts   (10)

─────────── **H** ───────────

handicap (han′ dē kap′) *n.* disadvantage; a race in which favorites are given a disadvantage (superior horses have to carry a greater weight)   (11)

harmony (här′ mə nē) *n.* getting on well together; agreement; pleasant and peaceful relationship   (8)

headlong (hed′ lông) *adv.* headfirst; carelessly; recklessly   (11)

heritage (her′ ə tij) *n.* something handed down from the past   (12)

─────────── **I** ───────────

illumination (i lü′ mə nā′ shən) *n.* amount of light; lighting up   (6)

immigrant (im′ ə grənt) *n.* a person who goes from one country to another to live   (12)

implement (im′ plə mənt) *n.* tool; device; utensil   (4)

inspire (in spīr′) *v.* to move towards some creative effort or act; fill with feeling or thought; influence   (12)

instrument (in′ strə mənt) *n.* a tool, implement, or device   (5)

intrepid (in trep′ id) *adj.* very brave; fearless   (7)

investigate (in ves′ tə gāt) *v.* to look into thoroughly; examine carefully; study   (5)

isolation (ī′ sə lā′ shən) *n.* being alone; separation from others   (2)

items (ī′ təmz) *n.* goods for sale; articles bought and sold; wares   (9)

---------- J ----------

jubilation (jü′ bə lā′ shən) *n.* rejoicing; celebration   (11)

---------- L ----------

laboratory (lab′ rə tôr′ ē) *n.* a place where scientific work is done; a room with special equipment for scientific investigation   (5)

leisure (lē′ zhər) *n.* time free from required work in which persons can do as they wish for enjoyment or just rest   (8)

---------- M ----------

marine (mə rēn′) *adj.* having to do with the sea; of the sea   (7)

merchandise (mėr′ chən dīz) *n.* goods for sale; articles bought or sold; wares   (9)

microscope (mī′ krə skōp) *n.* an instrument consisting of a combination of lenses for magnifying things that are too small for the naked eye to see   (5)

monument (mon′ yə mənt) *n.* something set up to keep alive the memory of a person or event, as a tablet, statue, or building   (12)

murky (mėr′ kē) *adj.* dark; gloomy; hazy   (7)

---------- O ----------

observation (ob′ zər vā′ shən) *n.* act of careful watching and studying   (5)

oriental (ôr′ ē en′ tl) *adj.* Eastern; relating to the countries of Asia as opposed to those of Europe and America   (6)

ornament (ôr′ nə mənt) *n.* decoration; a pretty object   (6)

---------- P ----------

pace (pās) *n.* rate of speed in walking or running; a step; type of step   (11)

panorama (pan′ ə ram′ ə) *n.* an unlimited or wide view   (2)

peer (pir) *v.* to look closely in order to see clearly   (5)

peril (per′ əl) *n.* danger; risk   (1)

physician (fə zish′ ən) *n.* medical doctor   (3)

picnic (pik′ nik) *n.* a meal in the open air, with food brought along   (8)

possessions (pə zesh′ ənz) *n.* things owned by a person   (3)

proceed (prə sēd′) *v.* to go; go on; continue   (1)

profession (prə fesh′ ən) *n.* an occupation requiring special and advanced training (doctor, nurse, lawyer, engineer, teacher)   (3)

propel (prə pel′) *v.* to push or push forward   (3)

protest (prə test′) *v.* to speak against; argue; object to   (1)

purchase (pėr′ chəs) *v*. to get by paying a price; buy   (9)

---------------- **R** ----------------

reckless (rek′ lis) *adj*. careless; irresponsible   (1)

record (ri kôrd′) *v*. to set down in writing to keep for future use   (5)

recreation (rek′ rē ā′ shən) *n*. play; amusement; games   (8)

recuperate (ri kü′ pə rāt′) *v*. to become well again after an illness or injury   (3)

refuge (ref′ yüj) *n*. place of safety or shelter   (12)

remedy (rem′ ə dē) *n*. any medicine or treatment that cures   (3)

---------------- **S** ----------------

schedule (skej′ ül) *n*. the times fixed for doing things; program   (4)

scientific (sī′ ən tif′ ik) *adj*. having to do with science or systems of knowledge based on observed facts and ideas tested by experiment   (5)

security (si kyùr′ ə tē) *n*. safety; the feeling of being safe   (10)

select (si lekt′) *v*. to pick out; choose   (9)

skillful (skil′ fəl) *adj*. having a special ability; being expert   (4)

solemn (sol′ əm) *adj*. serious; sad   (6)

solitary (sol′ ə ter′ ē) *adj*. alone; single; lonely   (6)

stamina (stam′ ə nə) *n*. lasting power; endurance   (11)

stationary (stā′ shə ner′ ē). *adj*. not moving; fixed in place   (1)

stroll (strōl) *v*. to take a quiet walk for pleasure   (8)

sturdy (stėr′ dē) *adj*. strong and firm   (10)

symbol (sim′ bəl) *n*. a particular object that stands for an idea or feeling   (12)

---------------- **T** ----------------

teamwork (tēm′ wėrk′) *n*. the acting together of two or more people; cooperation   (4)

tense (tens) *adj*. strained; nervous   (11)

timid (tim′ id) *adj*. easily frightened; fearful   (10)

toil (toil) *n*. hard, tiring work or labor   (2)

tourists (tùr′ ists) *n*. people who go on a trip for sightseeing and pleasure   (12)

tradition (trə dish′ ən) beliefs or customs handed down from the past   (6)

tranquil (trang′ kwəl) *adj*. peaceful; calm   (2)

triumph (trī′ umf) *n*. victory; success; achievement   (11)

---------------- **V** ----------------

variety (və rī′ ə tē) *n*. number of different kinds; lack of sameness   (9)

vegetation (vej′ ə tā′ shən) *n*. plant life; growing plants   (7)

vehicle (vē′ ə kəl) *n*. anything on wheels or runners for carrying people or things   (1)

visibility (viz′ ə bil′ ə tē) *n*. the degree to which things can be seen   (7)

volunteer (vol′ ən tir′) *n*. a person who does some work of his or her own free will, sometimes without pay   (3)

KEY TO PRONUNCIATION

The pronunciation of each word is shown just after the word, in this way:

ab bre vi ate (ə brē′ vē āt)

The letters and signs used are pronounced as in the words below.

The mark ′ is placed after a syllable with primary or heavy accent, as in the example above. The mark ′ after a syllable shows a secondary or lighter accent, as in **ab bre vi a tion** (ə brē′vē ā′ shən).

a	hat, cap	j	jam, enjoy	u	cup, butter
ā	age, face	k	kind, seek	u̇	full, put
ä	father, far	l	land, coal	ü	rule, move
		m	me, am		
b	bad, rob	n	no, in	v	very, save
ch	child, much	ng	long, bring	w	will, woman
d	did, red			y	young, yet
		o	hot, rock	z	zero, breeze
e	let, best	ō	open, go	zh	measure, seizure
ē	equal, be	ô	order, all		
ėr	term, learn	oi	oil, voice		
		ou	house, out	ə represents:	
f	fat, if			a in about	
g	go, bag	p	paper, cup	e in taken	
h	he, how	r	run, try	i in pencil	
		s	say, yes	o in lemon	
i	it, pin	sh	she, rush	u in circus	
ī	ice, five	t	tell, it		
		th	thin, both		
		ᵵH	then, smooth		